COOKING THE FANCY CUTS

TO PREPARE BRAINS

Soak for one hour in cool water, adding the juice of one-half lemon. Drain and then parboil for ten minutes. Drain and then trim free from excess tissue. Place under a weight to flatten and make firm, if desired, or cut into two and dip in flour and then in egg and finally in fine bread crumbs. Fry in hot fat until a golden brown. Serve with Hollandaise sauce.

ROAST SHOULDER OF VEAL

Have the butcher make a pocket in the veal for the filling. Now soak sufficient stale bread in cold water so that when pressed dry it will measure two cups. Place the bread in a saucepan and add

One cup of finely chopped onions,
Three tablespoons of finely chopped parsley,
One green pepper, chopped fine,
One-half cup of shortening.

Mix thoroughly and then cook slowly so that the onion does not brown. When tender add

One teaspoon of paprika,
Two teaspoons of salt,
One teaspoon of pepper.

Mix thoroughly and then cool and fill into veal. Sew the opening with a darning needle and a stout string or fasten with toothpicks. Dust the meat well with flour and then place in a hot oven to brown. Then reduce the heat of the oven to moderate and roast, allowing thirty minutes for the meat to start cooking and twenty-five minutes to the pound. Baste every ten minutes with:

One-half cup of vegetable salad oil in
One and one-half cups of boiling water.

CALF'S HEAR T A LA MODE

Wash and soak the heart for a few minutes in water and then remove the tubes, veins and cut the heart into dice. Parboil until tender. Then add, using sufficient water to cover

One half-cup of vinegar,
Four onions, chopped fine,
Two carrots, cut in dice,
One teaspoon of sweet marjoram,
Two teaspoons of salt,
One teaspoon of white pepper.

Thicken gravy and serve with toasted strips of bread.

Calf's heart may be cut in thin slices, dipped in flour and then fried. Calf's liver is most delicate and must be cooked quickly, either by panning or broiling. The head is used for mock-turtle soup or cooked and served with brown sauce or made into calves' head cheese. The tongue may be cooked until tender and then pickled in vinegar.

The feet may be used in place of the head for mock-turtle soup, and in place of the knuckle in making pepper pot.

TRIPE FRIED IN BA TTER

Cut the tripe into pieces the size of an oyster and then season and dip in a batter. Fry until golden brown in hot fat and then serve with Hollandaise sauce.

THE BA TTER

Break one egg in a cup and fill with milk. Place in a bowl and add

One and one-quarter cups of flour,

One teaspoon of salt,
One-half teaspoon of pepper.

Beat well to free from lumps.

CREOLE TRIPE

Mince four onions fine and then place in a saucepan, four tablespoonfuls of shortening; add the onions and cook until soft, but not brown. Now add four tablespoonfuls of flour. Stir to blend well and then add:

Two cups of strained tomatoes,
One green pepper, minced fine,
One-half pound of prepared mushrooms,
One pound of tripe cut into inch blocks.

Cook gently for twenty minutes and then season and serve.

PICKLED TRIPE

Cut the prepared tripe in strips one inch wide and two inches long and then place in a china bowl and add

Four onions cut in rings and parboiled,
Two bay leaves,
One dozen cloves,
Half-dozen allspice

and sufficient vinegar to cover. Let stand two days before using.

TURTLE AND SNAPPER

Lay the turtle on its back and cut off the head. Let turtle bleed for twenty minutes. Separate the body from the shell and remove the entrails. Carefully separate the liver and heart. Now, with a sharp knife, remove the meat from the shell and lay in boiling water for two minutes. Drain. Rub the legs and all flesh containing the outer skin until the skin is removed, with a coarse towel. Now, with a cleaver, chop the shell into five pieces and place in scalding water for five minutes. Remove from hot water. Use the knife to peel off the skin and bristle from the shell. Now lay the meat and shell in cold water for one and one-half hours. You now have white and green turtle meat ready to cook.

TO COOK

Put the meat and shell in a large preserving kettle with sufficient cold water to cover, adding

One pint jar of stewed tomatoes,
One stalk of celery,
One bunch of potherbs,
One bunch of parsley,
Three cloves,
Four allspice,
Four large onions,
Two bay leaves,
One medium-sized carrot,
Rind of one-half lemon,
Three tablespoons of Worcestershire sauce.

Tie the spices and vegetables in a piece of cheese-cloth and bring to a boil. Cook slowly until the meat is tender and then remove the white meat. Cook the green meat, most of which is in the shell, until it is tender. Place the meat, when tender, in cold water to blanch. Use the liquid for soup. Strain and add part of the turtle meat, hard-boiled egg, grated lemon rind and juice of lemon. Prepare the snapper same as green turtle. Only bleed snapper ten minutes.

SHRIMP SALAD

Open two tall cans of shrimp and then drain and wash under cold water. Now shred the coarse green outside leaves of lettuce very fine. Measure two cups and place in a bowl and add

One green pepper,
One onion, chopped very fine,

One-half cup of mayonnaise dressing.

Mix well and then fill into a nest of crisp lettuce leaves. Lay the shrimp on top and mask with mayonnaise. Garnish with two hard-boiled eggs into quarters.

SHRIMP

Shrimp come, as a rule, cooked, but to cook shrimp: Plunge the shrimp into boiler prepared as for crabs. Boil for ten minutes, then drain and cool. Remove the shells and then they may be used for salads, croquettes and fried shrimps.

TERRAPIN

Diamond back or salt water terrapin are best. Fresh water terrapin may be used for croquettes and puree. Clean the terrapin by placing in fresh water for six hours. Wash in warm water and then place them alive in boiling water. Cook for five minutes. Remove and then rub with a coarse cloth the neck, legs and tail to remove the skin. Wash again. Return to the pot. Cook until the legs leave the body easily. Usually about thirty-five minutes for small terrapin and seventy-five minutes for large ones. The age and condition determine the time of cooking. Cool. Now, before it is entirely cold, separate the terrapin from the shell, discard the small intestines, shell, gall, etc. Cut the meat into pieces.

Cook in cream sauce for a la Maryland; in brown sauce for a la mode or stewed terrapin.

STEWEDSNAPPER

Open a can of snapper into a china bowl and let stand for one hour; place in a saucepan.

Two cups of water,
Four tablespoons of cornstarch, dissolved in water,
Faggot of soup herbs,
Two cloves,

Two tablespoons of butter,
One and one-half teaspoons of salt,
One teaspoon of paprika,
Juice of one lemon,
Grated rind of one-fourth lemon.

Bring to a boil and cook slowly for fifteen minutes; then add the snapper meat, heat slowly 10 minutes, serve.

STEAKS

The selection of steak depends entirely upon the number of persons to be served. A steak cannot be classed as a cheap meat; the portions of bone and trimming makes this meat a rare luxury in these times of high prices.

Yet there come times when the men folk want steak—and steak it must be. There are three kinds of meats that are cut into steaks; namely, the loin, rump and round. All three will make delicious eating if properly prepared.

The round steak has the least waste, and if steaks are taken from the first three cuts they should be tender and juicy, providing they are cut sufficiently thick and are properly cooked.

The rump steak is fully as tender and palatable as loin and it contains about one-third less waste. The sirloin is the choicest cut in the whole carcass and it contains a proportionately large amount of waste.

Have the butcher cut the round steak one-half inch thick and then pound it with a meat ax to break the tough tissues. Place on a platter and brush with salad oil and let stand for one-half hour. Now broil in the usual manner, turning every four minutes. Lift to a hot platter and spread with choice meat butters given below.

Rump steak should be cut two inches thick and the bone and fat trimmed. Now nick and score the edge of the fat and brush with salad oil, and then broil the same as for round steak.

The sirloin steak should be cut two inches thick. Have the butcher remove the chine bone and then the flank end. Let him add a piece of suet to the flank end; then put it through the food chopper for hamburg steak. It is a mistake to cook the flank with the sirloin. Brush the steak with salad oil and then broil. Lift to a hot platter.

Place one pint of water and one tablespoonful of salt in the bottom of the broiling pan to prevent the fat drippings from taking fire. Turn the meat every four minutes, so that it makes the cooking even. To test the meat when broiling press with a knife; if it is soft and spongy it is raw. Watch carefully and when just beginning to become firm it is rare. Allow four minutes for medium and six minutes for well done.

Do not turn the meat with a fork. The intense heat has sealed or seared the surface and caused the meat to retain its juices, and if you use a fork to turn it you will puncture or make an opening so that these juices will escape.

A two-pound steak will be cooked rare in twelve minutes, medium in fifteen minutes and well done in eighteen minutes. Always lift to a hot platter.

FRENCHBUTTER

Two tablespoons of finely chopped chives,
One tablespoon of finely chopped leeks,
One tablespoon of finely chopped tarragon,
Juice of one-half lemon,
Two tablespoons of melted butter,
One-half teaspoon of salt,
One-half teaspoon of paprika.

Work to a smooth paste.

French and Italian and Swiss cooks frequently serve a vegetable garnish with steaks. It is prepared as follows:

One green pepper, chopped fine,
Two leeks, chopped fine,
Eight branches of parsley, chopped fine,
Two onions, chopped fine,
Ten branches of tarragon, chopped fine,
One-half cup of chives, chopped fine.

Place four tablespoonfuls of shortening or vegetable oil in a frying pan and add the herbs and cook very slowly until soft, taking care not to brown. Now season with salt, pepper and dress on a hot platter in a little mound at the bottom of the steak. Garnish with a slice of lemon.

ENGLISH BUTTER

One tablespoon of butter,
One-quarter teaspoon of white pepper,
One-quarter teaspoon of mustard,
One-half teaspoon of salt.

Work to a paste and then spread on a steak as soon as you place it on the platter.

LONDON BUTTER

One tablespoon of melted butter,
One tablespoon of Worcestershire sauce,
One-half teaspoon of salt,
One-half teaspoon of pepper,
One tablespoon of lemon juice.

Mix and then pour over the steak.

SWISS BUTTER

One tablespoon of grated onion,
One tablespoon of finely minced parsley,
One-half teaspoon of salt,

One-quarter teaspoon of paprika,
One and one-half tablespoons of butter.

Work to a smooth paste.

ITALIAN BUTTER

One green pepper, chopped very fine,
One teaspoon of paprika,
One-half teaspoon of salt,
Two tablespoons of butter.

Work to a smooth paste and then spread on the meat.

VEGETABLE GARNISH

Carrots, turnips and parsnips may be cut into cubes and then shaped like a cork. Cook until tender in boiling water and then brown quickly in a little hot fat. Beets and turnips may be cooked until tender and then scoop out the centres and fill with onions or cucumber mayonnaise.

BROILED HAMBURG STEAK

Do not fry or pan hamburg steak made from flank of sirloin. Place meat in bowl and add

Three-quarters cup of moist bread crumbs,
One onion, minced fine,
Two tablespoons of parsley,
One teaspoon of salt,
One-half teaspoon of paprika,
One egg.

Mix, form into flat cakes, brush with salad oil; place on baking dish. Broil in gas broiler for eight minutes, then place in hot oven for seven minutes longer. Spread with desired butter and send to the table in a baking dish. This will give a delicious flavored meat in place of the usual dry, tasteless cake that is frequently served.

SALADS

Salads are a popular summer dish. They should be made from fresh vegetables which contain the health-giving elements that are so vitally essential for our physical well-being. There are also the mineral salts which help purify the blood stream and thus keep us physically fit.

Eggs, etc., that are used in preparing the dressings have a food value that may be figured upon in our daily ration. Heavy salads, composed of meat, are best to be eliminated for the hot weather. Replace them with light, dainty, attractive salads, that are not only appetizing but also easily digested.

The making of a successful salad is an art indeed. The proper blending of the various ingredients and then using a well-blended dressing and garnishing, so that it will not only satisfy the eye but will tempt the palate as well; that is a real salad.

The proper combinations are very important; harmony must prevail. As, for instance, a combination of beets, tomatoes and carrots would not only be inartistic but also a poor combination of foods. Care must be taken in preparing the lettuce or other greens used. All plants that form into heads must be separately and thoroughly washed in order to free them from dirt and insects, and then they should be given a final washing in water that contains one tablespoon of salt to every two quarts, then rinsed in ice water. The bath in salt water will remove the tiny and almost invisible mites and slugs that cling to these greens.

Many varieties of salad dressing may be prepared from mayonnaise or from the dressing purchased in bottles. When the housewife fails to make a good mayonnaise dressing, or the family is small, a good standard dressing already prepared may be purchased and used in the following recipes:

RUSSIAN DRESSING

One cup of salad dressing, or mayonnaise,
One raw beet,
One raw carrot,

One raw onion.

Pare and then grate the vegetables into the salad dressing and then add:

One teaspoon of salt,
One teaspoon of paprika,
One tablespoon of sugar,
One-half teaspoon of mustard.

Beat to mix and then use. This dressing will keep for a week, if it is placed in a bottle and stored in a cool place.

FRENCH DRESSING

Place in a bottle:

One-half cup of salad oil,
Three tablespoons of vinegar or lemon juice,
One teaspoon of salt,
One-half teaspoon of mustard,
One-half teaspoon of pepper.

Shake until creamy and then store in a cool place. This will keep well until used.

ROQUEFORT DRESSING

One-half teaspoon of salt,
One-half teaspoon of paprika,
One tablespoon of Roquefort cheese,
One tablespoon of lemon juice,
Two tablespoons of salad oil.

Mix smooth and serve.

BOILED DRESSING

One cup of vinegar,

Three-quarters cup of water,
Three level tablespoons of cornstarch.

Dissolve the starch in the water and bring to a boil. Cook for five minutes and then add:

One well-beaten egg,
Four tablespoons of salad oil,
One teaspoon of mustard,
One and one-half teaspoons of salt,
One teaspoon of paprika,
Two teaspoons of sugar.

Beat till thoroughly mixed and then cook slowly for three minutes. Pour into jars or jelly glasses and thin out with cream or evaporated milk when using.

PIMENTO DRESSING

Add four finely chopped pimentoes to one-half cup of prepared salad dressing.

PAPRIKA DRESSING

Add one and one-half teaspoons of paprika to the French dressing. Shake well to blend. Paprika is a sweet, mild, red pepper that will not bite the tongue.

During the warm weather use salads twice a day, beginning the day with water-cress, radishes or crisp young onions or leaves of lettuce for your health's sake.

BLOND FRENCH DRESSING

Place in a wide mouthed bottle,

One teaspoon of sugar,
One teaspoon of mustard,

One-half teaspoon of salt,
Four tablespoons of white wine vinegar,
One-half cup of vegetable salad oil.

Shake until creamy.

The use of paprika is decidedly better than the pungent pepper. This pepper is mildly sweet-flavored spice that does not irritate the delicate lining of the throat or stomach. Now, fully as important as the green appetizers are the dainty salads, lettuce, corn salad, endive, romaine, tomatoes, onions, cucumbers, cabbage and the cooked vegetables, such as lima beans, peas, string beans, beets, etc.

The success of salads depends entirely on the dressings used with them. So, with this in mind, we will now prepare some delicious dressings. Place in a fruit jar and then put them in the ice box, where they can be had at a minute's notice.

You know that often when you come home just fagged out, when perhaps you did not take the time to get luncheon, a cool, crisp salad and some thinly sliced buttered bread and a cup of tea will not only satisfy and refresh you, but will also prevent a headache.

A LA MODE CANADIENNE

Shred the coarse green leaves of lettuce fine and then place in salad bowl and add:

Two cooked carrots,
Two cooked beets, cut in dice,
Two onions, chopped fine.

Toss gently to mix and then prepare the following dressing:

Place in fruit jar,

One-half cup of vegetable salad oil,
Two tablespoons of grated onion,

Four tablespoons of vinegar,
Three tablespoons of finely minced green or red pepper,
One teaspoon of paprika,
One and one-half teaspoons of salt,
Three-quarters teaspoon of mustard,
One-half cup of catsup or chili sauce.

Shake until well blended and then pour over the salad as you serve it.

TRY THIS DRESSING ON PLAIN LETTUCE

Wash and remove all blemishes from one bunch of scallions; then chop fine and add:

One-half cup of mayonnaise,
Two tablespoons of vinegar,
One and one-half teaspoons of salt,
One teaspoon of paprika,
One-half teaspoon of mustard.

Mix the spices and seasoning with the vinegar and add to the mayonnaise. Then add the finely chopped scallions. Serve on plain lettuce.

PARISIAN CELERY

Fill the grooves of the celery with highly seasoned cheese.

SCALLIONS A L'ITALIENNE

Wash and then remove the blemishes from two bunches of scallions, chop fine and then parboil and drain. Now cook four ounces of macaroni in boiling water until tender. Drain, blanch under cold water and then drain again. Now place the cooked macaroni and the prepared scallions in a saucepan and add:

One cup of brown gravy,
One cup of thick cream sauce,
One ounce of grated cheese,

Two teaspoons of salt,
One teaspoon of paprika.

Toss gently until hot and then serve with waffles in place of meat for luncheon.

PEA SHORE PIE

Grease a deep pudding pan well. Cut any variety of fish desired into pieces weighing about two ounces. Free from bones and skin and then roll in flour and place a layer of fish, then a layer of thinly sliced tomatoes, a layer of thinly sliced potatoes and then a layer of prepared fish. Season each layer with salt, pepper and finely chopped green peppers. Pour over it two cups of thick cream sauce with

One-half dozen clams,
One cup of cooked peas,
Two teaspoons of salt,
One teaspoon of paprika,
Two tablespoons of finely chopped parsley.

Cover with a crust rolled one-half inch thick. Bake in a moderate oven for one and one-quarter hours. Brush the pastry with milk and as soon as it browns lightly cover with a pie plate to prevent taking on too deep a color.

FISH SOUFFLE

This dainty dish is made by rubbing one-half cup of cold boiled fish through a fine sieve. Then add

One cup of cold cream sauce,
One tablespoon of salt,
One teaspoon of paprika,
One-half teaspoon of mustard,
Three tablespoons of finely chopped parsley,
One tablespoon of Worcestershire sauce,
Yolk of two eggs.

Beat hard to mix and then carefully fold in the stiffly beaten whites of two eggs. Pour into well-greased custard cups and then set the cups in a pan containing warm water, and bake in a moderate oven until firm in the centre, usually about twenty minutes.

FISH LOAF

Two cups of cold boiled fish,
One cup of prepared bread crumbs,
One cup of thick cream sauce,
One and one-half teaspoons of salt,
One teaspoon of paprika,
Two teaspoons of grated onions,
One green pepper, minced fine,
One well-beaten egg.

Mix and then pack into the prepared loaf-shaped pan. Stand this pan in a larger one containing hot water. Bake in a moderate oven for fifty minutes. Remove from the oven and let stand for a few minutes. Then unmould on a hot platter and serve with creole sauce.

To prepare the crumbs, soak stale bread in cold water; then place in a cloth and squeeze dry. Rub through a fine sieve and then measure.

To prepare the pan, grease the pan and then line it with a greased and floured paper.

BOILED SALT COD

Soak one and one-quarter pounds of boneless salt cod for four hours and then drain and wipe in a piece of cheese-cloth and plunge in a deep saucepan containing sufficient boiling water to cover the fish. Bring to a boil and then cook for thirty-five minutes. Lift and drain well and place on a hot platter. Cover with two cupfuls of cream sauce and garnish with one-quarter cupful of finely minced parsley and then sprinkle with two tablespoonfuls of grated cheese.

CONNECTICUT FISH CHOWDER

Any cheap fish that is fresh will do for this dish, or it may be made from the heads, fins and backbones of the fish, used for filets or broiling. Place the heads, fins and backbones of three medium-sized fish in a deep saucepan and add

Two quarts of cold water,
Two onions, cut fine,
One carrot, cut in tiny dice,
One-half bay leaf,
One-half teaspoon of thyme.

Cover and bring to a boil. Cook slowly for one hour. Now remove the heads, fins and backbones and pick the meat from the heads and backbones and return to the stock.

Now rub one cup of stewed tomatoes through a sieve and add five tablespoons of cornstarch. Stir until the starch is dissolved and then add to the stock. Bring quickly to a boil and add:

Two cups of diced and par-boiled potatoes,
Salt and pepper to taste,
Two tablespoons of butter,
Two tablespoons of finely chopped parsley.

Let boil up once and then serve. This is delicious. One pound of fish may be used in place of heads, fins and backbones.

FISH CUTLET

Place in a mixing bowl

Two cups of flaked cold fish,
One and one-half cups of prepared stale bread,
Two onions grated,
Four tablespoons of finely chopped parsley,
One tablespoon of salt,
One teaspoon of paprika,
One tablespoon of Worcestershire sauce,

One-half teaspoon of mustard,
One well-beaten egg.

Mix thoroughly and then shape into cutlets. Roll in flour and then dip in beaten egg, and then into fine bread crumbs. Fry in hot fat.

To prepare the bread, soak stale bread in warm water until soft. Place in a cloth and then squeeze until very dry; then rub through a colander to remove the lumps. Fish cutlets are served with a menu, as follows:

SALMON CHARTREUSE

Open a can of salmon and then drain. Remove the skin and bones and flake with a fork. Soak three tablespoons of gelatine in one-half cup of cold water and then place in a saucepan

Two tablespoons of finely chopped onion,
Two tablespoons of finely chopped parsley,
Two tablespoons of carrots,
Faggot of soup herbs,
Two cups of water.

Bring to a boil and cook slowly for ten minutes. Strain and then add

The juice of one-half lemon,
One and one-quarter teaspoons of salt,
One teaspoon of paprika,

and the dissolved gelatine.

Mix thoroughly and then cool and add the prepared salmon.

One tablespoon of grated onion,
Three tablespoons of finely chopped parsley.

Pour into a mould that has been rinsed with cold water and chilled on ice. Set in a cool place to mould. When ready to serve unmould on a bed of lettuce and serve with Russian dressing. This may be prepared Saturday afternoon.

BROILED SALT MACKEREL, FLEMISH STYLE

Soak the mackerel overnight in plenty of cold water to cover, keeping the skin side up. In the morning remove the head and then wash and parboil. Drain and then place on a baking dish and spread lightly with bacon or ham fat and dust lightly with flour. Place in the broiler of the gas range and broil until nicely browned. Now, while the mackerel is cooking, prepare a Flemish sauce as follows:

One onion,
One green pepper,
Two branches of parsley.

Chop very fine and then place in a saucepan with three tablespoons of butter. Cover closely and steam until the vegetables are soft. Now add:

One tablespoon of vinegar,
One teaspoon of sugar,
One-half teaspoon of mustard,
One teaspoon of pumpkin,
Two tablespoons of boiling water.

Bring to a boil and pour over the fish. Garnish with cress.

SALT COD, VERMONT

Select a thick centre; cut and soak for one hour in warm water. Wrap in a piece of cheese-cloth and plunge into boiling water. Boil for fifteen minutes and then drain. Divide into four individual baking dishes and cover with cream sauce. Sprinkle with fine bread crumbs and a little grated onion, and bake for ten minutes in a hot oven.

MEATS

In order to purchase meats intelligently so that we will receive the best value for money expended, it is necessary to know the nature of the cuts, and especially the proportionate amounts of lean meat, fat and bone that they contain; also the approximate food values of the meat obtained from various parts of the carcass.

HIND QUARTERS

Loin steak average 57 per cent. lean, 33 per cent. visible fat, 10 per cent. bone. Sirloin steaks in general contain a larger percentage of lean meat and a smaller amount of fat than the porterhouse or club steaks.

Rib cuts contain 52 per cent. lean meat, 31 per cent. fat, 17 per cent. bone. The greatest percentage of lean meat is found in the sixth rib, and the smallest in the eleventh and twelfth rib cuts.

Round steaks are meat cut from the round. They average 67 per cent. lean meat, 20 per cent. fat and 16 per cent. bone. The round steaks contain 73 per cent. to 84 per cent. lean meat.

The rump contains 49 per cent. lean meat, the round as a pot roast contains about 86 per cent. lean meat; the largest percentage of fat is found in the rump roast. Soup bones contain from 8 per cent. to 60 per cent. lean meat.

THE FOREQUARTERS

The forequarters of beef contain the chuck, the shoulder, clod, neck and shank. The chuck contains 67 per cent. lean meat, 20 per cent. fat and 12 per cent. bone. Chuck steak varies from 60 per cent. to 80 per cent. lean and from 8 per cent, to 24 per cent. fat.

The clod or bolar cut contains 82 per cent. lean meat and 5 per cent. bone.

Relatively more lean and less fat meat is found in the chuck rib roast than in the cut from the prime rib roast.

The navel, brisket and rib ends average 52 per cent. lean meat, 40 per cent. fat and 8 per cent. bone. The brisket and navel cuts are similar in proportion, while the rib ends slightly higher in percentage of bone and less lean.

Flank steak contains 85 per cent. lean meat and 15 per cent. fat. Shank cuts or soup bones from the shank vary from 15 per cent. to 67 per cent. lean meat and from 25 per cent. to 76 per cent. bone, while the boneless shank, used for stews, goulashes, hashes and minces, contain 85 per cent. lean meat and 15 per cent. fat.

The trimmings from the loin, in steaks reduce their weights about 13 per cent. and these trimmings average 4.6 per cent. fat and 2 per cent. bone. Round steak is reduced about 7 per cent. in weight in trimmings, principally in fat; chuck steaks about 6½ per cent., principally bone.

Rump, shoulder, pot roast and neck are all materially reduced in weight by fat and bone trimmings, the size and condition of the animal determining the actual amounts. The actual proportion of lean meat, fat and bone in the various cuts, their relative values of economy, fixes the prices to the consumer.

Taking the cuts of meat in their right order we have:

First, the neck for soup, stews and corning. The cost is very low and the waste is considerable.

Second, the chuck. This includes the entire shoulder and contains five ribs. The first two ribs are usually sold as shoulder, roast and steak, and while they are about the same quality as No. 9, they cost considerably less.

Third, the shoulder clod. This is part of the chuck and can be purchased in almost all markets. The price is low and there is no waste. It is used principally for steaks and pot roasts. When used for steaks, score the meat well.

Fourth, shank. According to the market price, this is the cheapest part of the beef. However, it contains 54 per cent. to 57 per cent. waste and requires long cooking. It is used for soups and stews.

Fifth, ribs. Contains eight ribs; five of these are the prime cuts and used for roasting exclusively.

Sixth, sirloin. The loin, some cuts contain as low as 3 per cent, waste. The sirloin is tender; therefore, quickly and easily cooked. For this reason it is one of the most popular cuts.

Seventh, porterhouse. This portion of the loin contains the choicest steaks, excellent and nutritious and easily cooked. The fillet or tenderloin forms a part of the loin and averages about 13 per cent. waste.

Eighth, rump. This cut is very nutritious, but requires careful cooking to render it tender; it contains slightly more waste than the round. Good steaks are obtained from the rump; it is also used for pot roast braising and coming.

Ninth, pin bone, the middle portion of the loin. It is of excellent quality, tender and of good flavor and quite as popular as the loin. It is the face cut of the rump.

Tenth, round. An inexpensive cut, containing only 7 per cent, waste. It is nutritious as tenderloin, but not as tender. The first essential in cooking is to sear the outside in order to retain the juices and then cook slowly until tender.

Steak and roast are cut from the round and the back or heel and is used for pot roast and stews.

One factor in helping to keep up the high prices of food is that the average woman, *when she goes to market, has in mind* fancy price and choice cuts for roast, steaks and chops. The choice cuts represent about 26 per cent. of the whole carcass, leaving about 74 per cent. to be disposed of. Now, if this becomes difficult, the fancy cuts must bear the additional cost and so become proportionately high in price.

Take a cross cut of beef, weighing about six pounds and wipe with a damp cloth, and one-half cupful of flour patted into it and then brown quickly on both sides in a frying pan and then place in a fireless cooker or a moderate oven together with

Two medium-sized onions,
One carrot, cut in quarters,
One and one-half cups of boiling water,

and cook slowly, allowing one-half hour for the meat to start cooking and then twenty-five minutes to the pound. Baste frequently. If baked in the range it should give a delicious, well-flavored roast, that will supply the most finicky family with a good substantial food.

The bolar cut from the shoulder may be prepared the same way.

Meat from the neck and shin may be used for stews, goulashes and meat loaves.

POT ROAST OF SHIN BEEF, ENGLISH STYLE

Have the butcher cut a piece of beef from the upper part of the shin, with the bone in. Wipe with a damp cloth and then pat in one-half cupful of flour. Brown quickly on both sides and then lift to a deep saucepan and add

One large turnip, cut in quarters,
One large carrot, cut in quarters,
One faggot of soup herbs,
One-half teaspoon of sweet marjoram,
Two cups of boiling water.

Cover closely and cook slowly until the meat is tender, allowing one-half hour for meat to start cooking and twenty-five minutes to the pound, counting the time when it is put into the kettle.

The plate and brisket may be used for soups, stews and goulashes and for corning. The brisket makes a splendid pot roast when boned and rolled. Also the plate or brisket may be used for à la mode.

The flank steak is a choice piece of lean, boneless meat that lies close to the ribs and weighs from one and three-quarters to two and one-half pounds. It may be used for steaks, if cut in slanting slices or for mock fillet or rolled or for hamburg steak.

When boiling or stewing meat, keep this in mind: Meat to be palatable and juicy must contain nutriment; it must be plunged into boiling water to seal the surface, by coagulating the albumen in the meat; and then it should be cooked just below the boiling point until tender, allowing one-half hour for the meat to heat and start cooking and then twenty-five minutes to the pound. Add salt just before removing from the fire.

Keep this fact in mind, that salt will, if added when the meat is just starting to cook, extract the juice.

For pot roast and braises, etc., it is necessary to quickly sear over the surface of the meat for the same reason that the meat was plunged into boiling water and then cook slowly, allowing the same proportion of time as for boiling or stewing.

The real object in cooking meat is to retain the juices and make it sufficiently to eat and increase its flavor.

BEEF STEW

Cut two and one-half pounds of stewing beef in two-inch pieces and then roll in flour and brown in hot fat; then add three pints of boiling water. Bring to a boil and cook slowly for one hour; then place in a saucepan

Two cups of flour,
One-half teaspoon of pepper,
One teaspoon of salt,
One tablespoon of baking powder.

Rub between the hands to mix and then add three-quarters cup of cold water to form a dough. Make into balls between the hands and then drop into the stew. Cover closely and boil fast for twelve minutes. Now remove the lid and cook for three minutes longer. Then season and serve.

TO PREPARE FISH FOR FRYING

Remove the head, fins and bones, using them for the fish stock. Place fillets in a dish and marinate for one hour in

Three tablespoons of lemon juice or vinegar,
Two tablespoons of salad oil,
Two tablespoons of grated onion,
One teaspoon of salt,
One teaspoon of paprika.

Then roll lightly in flour and dip into beaten egg, then in fine crumbs and fry until golden brown in hot fat.

GRILLED FISH

Sea trout, striped bass or other fish may be used. Clean and bone the fish and then place in baking dish and spread freely with salad oil. Broil for twelve minutes in broiler of the gas range or bake for fifteen minutes in a hot oven. Serve with a fish sauce prepared as follows:

Chop fine

Four onions,
Three large tomatoes,
Two green peppers.

Now chop two ounces of salt pork or fat bacon very fine and place in a skillet and cook until nicely browned. Add the finely chopped onions and tomatoes and green pepper and cook slowly until the vegetables are soft. Then season with

One-half teaspoon of sugar,
One teaspoon of salt,
One-half teaspoon of white pepper,
Juice of one-half lemon.

Mix thoroughly and serve with the fish.

FISH LOAF

Prepare a sauce as follows:

Place in a saucepan

One cup of milk,
Five tablespoons of flour.

Stir with a fork until the flour is dissolved and then bring quickly to a boil. Cook three minutes and then remove and pour into a mixing bowl, and add

Two cups of cold-boiled fish,
One cup of cold-boiled rice,
One cup of stale bread, prepared as for fish cutlet,
Four tablespoons of shortening (finely chopped salt pork if desired),
One large onion,
One large green pepper,
Six branches of parsley, minced very fine,
One tablespoon of paprika,
One-half teaspoon of mustard,
One tablespoon of Worcestershire sauce,
One-half teaspoon of sweet marjoram,
One egg.

Beat hard to thoroughly mix and then pour into a well-greased and floured loaf-shaped pan. Place this pan in a larger one containing hot water. Bake in a moderate oven for one hour. Serve with a sauce made as follows:

Two cups of stewed tomatoes,
Four onions, chopped fine,
One green pepper, chopped fine.

Cook until onions and peppers are soft and then rub through a coarse sieve. Now add

One-half cup of water,
Three tablespoons of cornstarch,

Two teaspoons of salt,
One teaspoon of sugar,
One-half teaspoon of pepper,
Pinch of cloves.

Mix well and then pour into tomato mixture. Stir well until the boiling point is reached and then cook three minutes. Add two tablespoons of butter and serve.

BROILED BASS

Have the fish dealer split the bass for broiling, then wash and pat dry with a paper napkin and cover the cut surface of the fish with salad oil. Place on a baking sheet and broil in the broiler of the gas range until nicely browned; then set in the oven for five minutes to finish cooking.

CREAM FINNAN HADDIE

Cover the fish with cold water and then bring to a boil. Drain and cover with cream sauce. Now add:

One green pepper, chopped fine,
One onion grated,
Five tablespoons of finely chopped parsley,
Two tablespoons of butter.

Simmer slowly for ten minutes to cook the herbs; then lift to the toast.

LONG ISLAND SOUND COCKTAIL

Place in a bowl

One-half bottle of tomato catsup,
One tablespoon of grated onion,
Two tablespoons of finely minced parsley,
One tablespoon of finely minced green pepper,
One tablespoon of Worcestershire sauce,
One-half teaspoon of mustard.

Mix well and then take the clam shells and scrub them clean. Fill with a mixture as follows:

One cup of cold-boiled fish,
One onion, chopped fine,
One green pepper, chopped fine.

Mix well. Make a well in the centre and fill with a sauce. Dust with paprika and serve ice cold.

FILET FISH, SOUTHERN STYLE

Clean, wash and drain fish. Do not dry. Have fat smoking hot. Place fish in pan, reduce heat and cook slowly until brown and crisp.

FISH CAKES

Boil fifteen large potatoes and then mash fine and add

One-half pound of prepared shredded codfish,
One egg,
Lump of butter the size of an egg,
One teaspoon of paprika.

Mix thoroughly and then form into balls. Roll in flour and fry until golden brown in hot fat.

COLD SPICE TONGUE

Select a medium-sized tongue without the gullet and wash well; then soak for four hours in warm water. Place in a deep saucepan and cover with warm water and add

One carrot, cut in dice,
Two onions sliced,
One faggot of soup herbs,
Two bay leaves,
Two allspice,

Four cloves,
One cup of strong cider vinegar.

Cover closely and bring to a boil; then simmer and keep just below the boiling point for three hours. Let cool in the liquid and then, when cold, chill in the ice box before slicing.

The coarse left-over parts of the tongue may be used for meat loaf, croquettes or hash.

PICKLED TRIPE

Cut one pound of cooked honeycomb tripe in pieces one inch by three inches. Place in a casserole dish and add

One cup of vinegar,
One-half cup of water,
One onion, cut fine,
One teaspoon of salt,
One-half teaspoon of white pepper,
One bay loaf,
Eight cloves,
Ten allspices,
One small red pepper pod.

Cover and bake in hot oven for thirty minutes and then cool.

BAKED HAM, VIRGINIA

Scrub a small ham and cook until tender. The fireless cooker will prevent the ham from wasting while cooking. When tender, lift and remove the skin. Trim to shape and then place in a bowl

Three-quarters cup of brown sugar,
One-quarter cup of cinnamon,
One teaspoon of nutmeg,
One teaspoon of cloves,
One teaspoon of allspice.

Mix thoroughly and then pat and rub into the ham. Place in a hot oven and bake for forty minutes, basting frequently with one-half cupful of water and one-half cupful of vinegar.

CORN BEEF HASH

Cut the cooked meat into one-half inch cubes and place in a saucepan and add to each cup of meat

One and one-half cups of pared and diced potatoes,
One-half cup of finely chopped onions,
One cup of boiling water.

Cover closely and steam until meat and potatoes are tender and the water is evaporated; then season. Now melt three tablespoons of shortening in an iron frying pan and when hot turn in the hash, forming an omelet shape in half the pan. When nicely browned, turn the hash with a cake turner, still keeping the omelet shape, and brown. Turn on a hot platter and garnish with finely chopped parsley.

BROWN POT ROAST OF SHIN BEEF

Wipe the meat with a damp cloth and then pat into it one-half cup of flour. Now heat the bacon fat left from cooking the bacon for breakfast in a saucepan and place in the meat. Brown quickly, turning frequently until every part is nicely browned; then add two cups of water and cover closely and cook slowly for one hour. Now add

Four medium-sized carrots,
Four medium-sized onions.

Season and cover again and cook slowly until the meat and vegetables are tender, usually about thirty-five minutes. Now add sufficient water to make one and three-quarter cups of gravy.

Prepare the dumpling as follows: Place one quart of boiling water in a saucepan and add one teaspoon of salt. Place in a mixing bowl

One and one-half cups of flour,
One teaspoon of salt,
One-quarter teaspoon of pepper,
Two teaspoons of baking powder,
One onion, grated,
One teaspoon of shortening.

Mix thoroughly and then add one-half cup of water. Form to a dough and drop by the teaspoonful into the boiling water. Cover the saucepan closely and cook for fifteen minutes; then lift on a warm dish and place the dumpling as a border around the platter. Lift the meat and vegetables in the centre and pour the gravy over all.

VIRGINIA SAUCE

Strain the liquid from the pan in which the ham was baked and add one-half cupful of flour. Brown well and then add

Two and one-half cups of the liquid from the pan,
One cup of vinegar,
One-half cup of syrup,
Two teaspoons of salt,
One teaspoon of paprika,
One-half teaspoon of nutmeg.

Bring to a boil and cook for ten minutes. Now strain into a gravy bowl and serve.

PORK TENDERLOIN

One and a half pounds of pork tenderloins will make eight nice-sized fillets. Place on a platter and baste with

One small onion, minced fine,
Three tablespoons of lemon juice,
Two tablespoons of salad oil,
One teaspoon of salt,
One teaspoon of paprika.

Turn the fillet to marinate and when ready to cook lift and roll lightly in flour and then dip in beaten egg and then into fine bread crumbs. Cook until golden brown in hot fat.

ROAST FRESH HAM

Select a small baby pig ham and have the butcher bone and then leave space for the filling. Wipe with a damp cloth and then prepare and fill with highly seasoned bread crumbs. Tie into shape and then dust with flour and place in a baking dish and put in a hot oven to brown. Then reduce the heat and baste frequently with hot water, allowing the ham thirty minutes to start and the meat cooking thirty minutes to the pound after that. When ready to serve, lift to a warm platter and garnish with parsley or water-cress and serve with Virginia sauce. Place one medium-sized apple in with the ham to bake.

BRAISED ROLLED FLANK STEAK

Have the butcher score and trim the steak. Now soak sufficient stale bread in cold water to soften. Press dry and then rub through a fine sieve. Measure and place two cupfuls in the mixing bowl and add

Four tablespoons of shortening,
One cup of finely chopped onions,
One bunch of potherbs, chopped fine,
One level tablespoon of salt,
One level teaspoon of pepper.

Mix well and then spread on a steak and roll. Tie securely with a stout string and then pat three-quarters cup of flour into the meat. Melt four tablespoons of shortening in a deep saucepan and when smoking hot add the prepared meat. Brown the meat, turning frequently, and then, when nicely brown, add one cupful of boiling water and simmer slowly, allowing the meat one-half hour to start cooking and thirty minutes to the pound. Add four large onions and when ready to lift one cup of boiling water for gravy. Usually this gravy requires no thickening.

PLANKED STEAK

Have the butcher cut the steak in two and one-half inch thicknesses from the large end of the sirloin. Remove the flank end and then the tenderloin, also taking out the bones. The butcher will do this for you. Now, when ready to prepare the steak, soak the plank in cold water for one hour. Heat the broiler and then place the plank in the oven. Cook the steak until quite rare in the broiler and then lift to a hot plank. Prepare a border of mashed potatoes and put them in a pastry bag, forced out around the edge of the plank. Garnish and smother with onions and minced green peppers. Place in a hot oven for ten minutes. Use the tenderloin for minute steaks. Hamburg the flank and serve hamburg steaks.

LIVER AND BACON, CREOLE

Have the butcher cut the liver in thin slices. Wipe with a clean damp cloth and then roll in flour and brown in hot fat. Now add

One cup of stewed tomatoes,
One and one-half cups of thinly sliced onions,
Two green peppers, chopped fine.

Cover closely and cook for five minutes, then add

Two tablespoons of cornstarch,
One and one-half teaspoons of salt,
One teaspoon of paprika,
One-quarter teaspoon of mustard,
One-half cup of cold water.

Dissolve the starch and spices well and then bring the mixture to a boil and cook slowly for fifteen minutes. Now place mashed potatoes on a large platter, shaping them flat on top. Lay the slices of liver on and then pour over them the sauce and garnish with nicely brown strips of bacon. Sprinkle with finely chopped parsley and serve.

CHOP SUEY

Slice sufficient meat from the cold roast of pork. Now cut in half-inch blocks and place in a pan and add

One cup of celery, cut in dice,
One green pepper, minced fine,
Four onions, minced fine,
One cup of finely shredded cabbage,
One and one-half cups of thick brown sauce,
Two teaspoons of salt,
One teaspoon of pepper,
One teaspoon of Worcestershire sauce.

Heat slowly to the boiling point and cook until the celery and cabbage are tender and then make a border around a large hot platter of cooked noodles and lift on the chop suey. Garnish with finely chopped parsley and serve.

Note.—Make the brown sauce from the left-over gravy and bones making a stock.

DELMONICO ROAST BEEF

Have the butcher cut the seventh and eighth rib from a roast, removing the chine bone. Now have him remove the blade and meat between it and the skin, cutting off the top of the ribs. This gives you a heart-shaped piece of very tender beef. It is really the eye of these two ribs. Place the roast in a pan and dust lightly with flour, and then place in a hot oven for thirty minutes to start cooking. Now reduce the heat and cook, allowing twenty minutes to the pound, counting the time from the minute you reduce the heat.

Use the top of the ribs and the piece of meat from the blade for the pot roast or a beef à la mode. Have the butcher remove the blade and roll the flap-like piece around the ribs, fastening it with a skewer or the entire piece may be boned and rolled.

BAKED SLICE OF HAM

Have the butcher cut the ham in one-inch thick slices. Trim and then cut around the edges every two inches apart to prevent curling. Place on a baking dish and pour over the ham

One cup of water,
Two tablespoons of syrup.

Bake in slow oven 25 minutes.

ROAST SHOULDER OF LAMB

Have the butcher bone and roll the shoulder and then when ready to use wipe with a damp cloth and pack with the following mixture: Chop very fine

Three onions,
Four branches of parsley,

One leek.

Pat with flour and then roast in the oven, allowing thirty minutes to start cooking and twenty minutes to the pound, gross weight. Baste the meat after it commences to brown with one and one-half cups of boiling water.

The season for spring lamb is from January to July. The meat is delicate and while less nutritious than mutton is delicious.

Yearling is a splendid choice for lamb. It is fully as nutritious as mutton, without the excess fat of mutton. Fat mutton frequently disagrees with persons of delicate digestion and therefore should be discarded from the menu, and the yearling should be substituted.

The choice mutton is raised in Virginia, Pennsylvania and North Carolina, while that which comes from Wisconsin is of splendid quality. Canada also sends us some fine meat.

Prime mutton is large and heavy, the fat firm and white and the flesh a deep red in color and very finely grained. This meat contains fully as much nutriment as beef.

Soups and broths made from mutton when the fat is removed are very wholesome and are frequently ordered in diets by physicians. Mutton should be hung for a short period to ripen, but lamb should be used a short time after it is dressed.

The cuts in the side of lamb or mutton usually number six: (1) The neck, (2) the chuck, which includes some of the ribs as far as the shoulder blade, (3) the shoulder, (4) the flank or breast, (5) the loin and (6) the leg.

In some parts of the country the butcher makes a cut, using the rack end of the loin and chuck for making the rib or French chops. The term chops is intended to designate meat cut from the rack or loin into chops, preferably one and one-quarter inches thick. Where the meat is cut with nine ribs on the loin, the shoulder and balance of the chuck is cut into chops for panning or braising. These chops require longer time for cooking than those cut from the rack or loin.

ACCOMPANIMENTS FOR LAMB AND MUTTON

Serve with a roast shoulder or leg of lamb, mint sauce, green grape jelly, peas or asparagus and baked potatoes. With mutton or lamb chops serve green grape jelly, mint or currant jelly.

Mutton may be boiled and served with caper or soubis (onions) sauces, currant jelly sauce, boiled or mashed potatoes, peas, string beans, asparagus, stuffed tomatoes and cole slaw.

HOW TO DISTINGUISH BETWEEN LAMB AND MUTTON

Look first at the joint above the hoof. In lamb this joint is serrated or tooth-shaped when broken, while in the yearling and mutton it is the smooth oval ball-and-socket joint. In lamb the bones are pinkish in color; in mutton the bones are a blue-white color. The pinkish colored skin should be removed from lamb and yearling before cooking. This skin contains the woolly flavor.

BONE AND STUFFED SHOULDER OF LAMB

Have the butcher bone the shoulder of lamb and then wipe with a damp cloth. Now prepare a filling as follows: Mince fine sufficient parsley to measure one-half cup. Place in a bowl and add

One green pepper, minced fine,
Two onions, minced fine,
One cup of fine bread crumbs,
Two teaspoons of salt,
One teaspoon of pepper,
One-half teaspoon of sweet marjoram.

Mix and then spread the filling and roll, tying securely. Now pat just sufficient flour into the meat to cover. Place on a rack in the baking pan and put in a hot oven. Just as soon as the meat becomes brown commence the basting with one cup of boiling water. Reduce the heat to a moderate oven.

The time to cook: Allow the meat thirty minutes for heating, so as to start cooking, and then twenty minutes to the pound, counting gross weight.

Keep the fact in mind that the rolled and filled meat requires more time than just the plain shoulder.

To roast the shoulder unboned allow one-half hour to start cooking and then fifteen minutes to the pound.

The leg of lamb may be boned and rolled or rolled and filled, and then cooked just like the shoulder.

BENGAL CURRY OF LAMB

Use the broken and coarse pieces of meat from the roast lamb. Chop fine and then place in a saucepan and add just sufficient water to barely cover. Now add

One onion, minced fine,
One green pepper, minced fine,
Four branches of parsley.

Cook slowly until the meat is very tender. Now thicken the gravy, using cornstarch, and season with

One teaspoon of Worcestershire sauce,
Four tablespoons of catsup,
Two teaspoons of salt,
One teaspoon of paprika,
One-half teaspoon of curry powder.

Make a border of cooked rice on a hot platter. Lift the curry into the centre of platter and garnish with one hard-boiled egg, chopped fine.

BAKED EMINCE OF LAMB IN GREEN PEPPERS

Mince the left-over portion of roast lamb fine, then measure and add any filling that may be left over. Place in a saucepan and add just sufficient boiling water to cover. Cook slowly until tender and then thicken the gravy. Now to one cup of the cold meat add

One cup of boiled rice,
One cup of canned tomatoes,
Three onions, chopped fine,
One tablespoon of salt,
One teaspoon of paprika.

Mix and then fill into the prepared peppers. Set in a baking pan and add one cup of boiling water. Bake in a moderate oven for thirty-five minutes. Serve with cheese sauce. Boiled mutton or lamb may be used in these dishes to replace the roast meat.

HOW TO USE LEFT OVER LAMB

Cut slices from the roast lamb and then line a large platter with crisp leaves of lettuce. Place on the platter the slices of meat. Serve with mint or currant jelly. Use the uneven pieces for curry of lamb or a baked emince of lamb, with green peppers and vegetable salad.

LAMB BOILED WITH RAVOLI

Have the butcher cut for stewing one pound of the neck of lamb. Wash and place in a saucepan and add

Three pints of cold water,
One faggot of soup herbs,
One carrot, cut very fine,
Two onions, chopped fine.

Cook very slowly until the meat is tender and then strain off the broth. Cool, then pick the meat from the bones. Chop the meat very fine and add

One and one-half teaspoons of salt,
One teaspoon of paprika,
Two onions, grated,
One green pepper, chopped fine,

One egg.

Mix thoroughly and then prepare a dough as follows: Place in a mixing bowl

Two cups of flour,
One teaspoon of salt,
One teaspoon of paprika,
Three tablespoons of finely minced parsley.

Mix by rubbing between the hands and then use one large egg and five tablespoons of water to make a dough. Knead until very smooth and then roll out as thin as paper. Cut into four-inch squares and brush the edges with water. Place a spoonful of prepared meat on the dough and then fold over and press the wet edges of the pastry tightly together. When all are ready drop in a large saucepan of boiling water. Cook for fifteen minutes and then lift with a skimmer; place in a dish and pour over the heated and seasoned lamb broth; then sprinkle over all four tablespoons of grated cheese and two tablespoons of finely minced parsley.

LAMB HARICOT

Soak one pint of lima beans overnight and then look over carefully in the morning. Parboil and then place in a baking dish with

One-half cup of diced onions,
One pound of neck of mutton cut into cutlets,
One cup of canned tomatoes.

Season with salt and pepper and add sufficient boiling water to cover all. Place in a moderate oven and bake for three hours.

INDIVIDUAL LAMB POTPIES

Mince the meat left on the leg of lamb. Place in a saucepan and cover with cold water, adding

One carrot, diced,

Four onions,
Four potatoes cut in halves.

Cook slowly until the vegetables are soft; lift the onions and potatoes and thicken the gravy and season with

Two teaspoons of salt,
One teaspoon of pepper,
One green pepper, chopped fine,
One tablespoon of Worcestershire sauce.

Place portion of the meat, two potatoes, one onion and some gravy in individual baking dishes. Cover with a crust of pastry and bake in a moderate oven for twenty minutes.

SPANISH MACARONI

Mince fine

Three green peppers,
Four onions,
Two tomatoes.

Now place five tablespoons of fat in a frying pan and add the prepared vegetables and cook slowly until tender without browning, and then add one-half package of cooked macaroni and

Two teaspoons of salt,
One teaspoon of pepper,
One-half cup of gravy from the kidney stew.

Cook slowly for fifteen minutes.

FALL MENU

BREAKFAST
Oranges
Cereal and Cream

Creamed Beef in Popover Cases
Coffee

DINNER
Radishes   Sliced Cucumbers
Kidney Pie
Spanish Macaroni   Buttered Beets
Cole Slaw
Orange Pudding   Coffee

SUPPER
Rice Croquettes with Cream Beef
Sauce
Cole Slaw
Orange Shortcake   Tea

HOW TO PREPARE RECIPES

POPOVERS

Place the popover pans in the oven to heat. Break one egg in a measuring cup and then fill with milk and turn into the mixing bowl and add

One-half teaspoon of salt,
One cup of sifted flour.

Beat with a Dover egg-beater for five minutes and then remove the smoking hot popover pans from the oven and grease well. Pour in the batter and place at once in a hot oven and bake for thirty-five minutes. Do not open the oven door for ten minutes after the popovers are placed in the oven. When the popovers are twenty-five minutes in the oven, turn down the gas and then bake slowly to thoroughly dry out for the balance of the time allowed for baking.

This amount will make eight small or six large popovers. Now, while the popovers are baking, the creamed beef can be prepared. Cut one-quarter pound of dried beef fine, using a pair of scissors to cut with. Place in a pan and cover with boiling water and let stand for five minutes. Drain and then make a cream sauce as follows:

Place one and one-half cups of milk in a saucepan and add six tablespoons of flour and stir to dissolve, and then bring to a boil and cook for three minutes. Add the prepared dried beef and two tablespoons of finely minced parsley and let simmer slowly until the popovers are ready.

Cut a slice from the tops of the popovers and fill them with the prepared creamed beef. Place a tiny dot of butter on top of each popover and dust lightly with paprika.

KIDNEY PIE

The meat pie can be made to be an economical dish. These pies are served in the Chelsea Coffee House in London.

Remove the fat and tubes from one large beef kidney and then cut into pieces the size of a walnut. Place in a saucepan and add three cups of boiling water and let simmer slowly for ten minutes. Turn into a colander and let the cold water run on the kidney for five minutes. Now return the kidney to the saucepan and add

One-half teaspoon of thyme,
One-half teaspoon of sweet marjoram,
Four onions, cut in pieces.

Cook slowly until tender and then add sufficient boiling water to cover. Add the dumplings, made as follows: Strain gravy from the kidney and add sufficient water to measure three and one-half cups. Place in a saucepan and when boiling add the dumplings, made as follows. Place in a mixing bowl

One cup of mashed potatoes,
One cup of flour,
One tablespoon of baking powder,
One teaspoon of salt,
One teaspoon of paprika,

Three tablespoons of grated onion,
Two tablespoons of finely-minced parsley,
One egg.

Work to a smooth paste and then form into balls the size of a large walnut, and drop into the prepared stock and cook for ten minutes. Lift and thicken the gravy slightly. Now make a pastry as follows:

Three cups of flour,
One teaspoon of salt,
Two teaspoons of baking powder.

Sift and then add the one-half pound of finely chopped suet and rub it into the flour well. Mix to a dough with two-thirds cup of water and roll out one-quarter inch thick on a floured pastry board. Line a large baking dish or individual custard cups. Now put a layer of kidney in the bottom and season with salt, pepper and finely minced onion. Place a dumpling on top and then a layer of thinly sliced hard-boiled egg. Cover with well-seasoned gravy and then with a crust, brushing the edges of the crust well with water. Now cut two gashes in the top of the crust to permit the steam to escape and then brush the top with water. If a large pie, bake for one hour; if individual ones, bake in a moderate oven for thirty-five minutes. Use three eggs in the kidney pie.

ORANGE PUDDING

Place in a mixing bowl

One-half cup of sugar,
Yolk of one egg,
Four tablespoons of shortening.

Cream well and then add the juice and pulp of two oranges, which should measure three-quarters cup, and

One and one-quarter cup of flour,
Three teaspoons of baking powder.

Beat to mix and then turn into well-greased and floured mould and cover the mould. Boil for one hour and then serve with the following sauce:

Three-quarters cup of sugar,
One-half cup of water,
Juice of one orange,
Grated rind of one orange,
Two tablespoons of cornstarch.

Stir to dissolve the sugar and starch and then bring to a boil and cook for three minutes and serve.

RICE CROQUETTES WITH CREAM BEEF

Mould well-seasoned cooked rice into croquettes; then dip and flour and brown in hot fat.

Make a cream sauce as follows: Place in a saucepan

Two cups of milk,
One-half cup of flour.

Stir to dissolve the flour and then bring to a boil and cook slowly for five minutes. Add one-half pound of dried beef, prepared as for breakfast, and serve with the croquettes.

ORANGE SHORT CAKE

Place in a mixing bowl

One cup of flour,
One-half teaspoon of salt,
Two teaspoons of baking powder,
Five tablespoons of sugar,
One-half cup of water.

Beat to a stiff dough and then spread on a well-greased and floured layer-cake pan, making the dough higher at the sides than in the middle of the pan. Cover with sliced oranges, cut into small pieces with a sharp knife. Now place in a bowl:

Six tablespoons of brown sugar,
Two tablespoons of flour,
One-half teaspoon of nutmeg.

Mix well and then spread on the shortcake and bake in a moderate oven for thirty minutes. Much of the actual preparation of the menu can be prepared on Saturday.

Use yolk of one egg for making dressing for coleslaw. For orange cake use

White of one egg,
One-half glass of jelly.

Place in a bowl and beat until mixture holds its shape. Pile on orange shortcake.

HALLOWE'EN

On Hallowe'en the good fairies are permitted to make themselves visible to their many friends—so the traditions of Ireland tell us. And the little ones, as they are called by the romantic fun-loving Irish nation, play a great many tricks this night on their enemies and they reward their true friends with many blessings.

It is truly a wonderful night for the romantic maiden to delve into the future and find, or try to find, her luck when seeking for the knowledge of her future life partner. In those good old days of long ago, the lad and lassie spent a pleasant evening trying all the lucky spells to insure them success in their love affairs for the coming year.

And in the midst of much hilarity many games are played; there are bobbing and ducking for apples, spinning the plate, post-office, heavy, heavy, what hangs over and forfeits. These were some of the old-fashioned ways the boys and girls of yesteryear passed a happy evening.

Other old legends told that this one night in the year the spooks or ghosts were permitted to roam the earth, so that, to escape their notice, all must go masked—hence our young folk disguised themselves and wandered forth from house to house, seeking entertainment; for many informal parties were held on this eve and no one was refused admission; each visitor was treated to apples and nuts and then he wandered on his way.

Let your young folk entertain their friends with a good old-fashioned Hallowe'en party; let them play the old games of long ago, and then close to the magic hour of midnight serve a real old-fashioned Hallowe'en supper.

SOME SUGGESTIVE MENUS

No. 1.
Cider
Salted Nuts Olives
Sardines and Potato Salad
Jack o' Lantern Cakes Coffee

No. 2.
Cider Cup
Radishes Celery
Gloucester Cod a la King
Cheese Sandwiches
Fruit Cakes Coffee
Nuts Raisins Apples

No. 3.
Celery Salted Nuts
Baked Virginia Ham
Potato and Pepper Salad
Rolls Butter
Ice Cream Coffee

No. 4.

        Radishes   Home-made Pickles
Fried Oysters
Potato and Celery Salad
Rolls and Butter
Fruit Ginger Bread   Coffee

Have corn husks and pumpkins for the decorations; use autumn leaves, strung together, for wall decorations. Cover the table with a silence cloth and then with linen table cloth, and place in the centre of the table a new wooden pail filled with cider. Bank the sides of the pail with corn husk, golden ears of corn and autumn leaves.

Now wire the handle so that it will be in an upright position. Wrap the handle with yellow tissue paper and fasten a small jack o'lantern made from a small pumpkin to the handle, so that it will hang in the well of the bucket. Arrange the table in the usual manner. Serve the cider from this well during the supper.

Hollow out a medium-sized pumpkin and cut in it a jack o' lantern and set bowls in the pumpkins to hold the radishes, pickle and sandwiches, sugar, etc., and make tiny pumpkins from the yellow crêpe paper, filling them with hard candies for souvenirs.

HOW TO MAKE THE CIDER CUP

Place in a large bowl some crushed ice and

One gallon of cider,
Three bananas, cut into thin slices,
Two oranges, cut into thin slices,
Three baked apples, cut into bits.

Mix and then serve.

SARDINE AND POTATO SALAD

(Twenty-five Persons)

Wash and then cook eight pounds of potatoes until tender and then, when cool, peel and cut into thin slices into a large mixing bowl. Now add

One cup of finely chopped onions,
One-half cup of finely chopped parsley,
One cup of finely chopped green peppers,
Two cups of finely chopped celery,
Two cups of mayonnaise or cooked dressing,
One-half cup of vinegar,
One tablespoon of salt,
One teaspoon of pepper,
One and one-half teaspoons of mustard.

Toss to mix thoroughly and then prepare individual nests of lettuce and place three-quarters cup of the potato salad in each nest. Mould it into a cone and then lay four sardines, tail end up, against the salad. Garnish with finely chopped parsley and serve.

JACK O' LANTERN CAKES

Bake a sponge cake in individual or muffin pans and then ice with chocolate water icing and make the lantern face with white icing.

GLOUCESTER COD A LA KING

(Twelve Persons)

Select a three-pound piece of boneless salt cod from the center cut; soak for three hours and then place in a piece of cheese-cloth and tie loosely, plunge into boiling water and boil for thirty minutes. Drain. Place two quarts of milk in a saucepan and add one and one-half cups of flour. Stir with a wire spoon to dissolve the flour and then bring to a boil and cook slowly for ten minutes. Now add

Two well beaten eggs,
The prepared fish, broken into flakes with a fork,
Juice of one lemon,
Two green peppers, cut into pieces and parboiled,

One tablespoon of grated onion,
One teaspoon of paprika.

Heat slowly until very hot and then serve on toast.

FRUIT CAKE

Place in a mixing bowl

Two and one-half cups of syrup,
One cup of shortening.

Cream well and then add

Eight cups of flour,
Four level tablespoons of baking powder,
One cup of milk,
One-half cup of cocoa,
One tablespoon of cinnamon,
One teaspoon of cloves,
One teaspoon of allspice,
Two eggs,
Two cups of finely-chopped peanuts.

Beat to mix thoroughly and then grease and flour a baking pan and turn in the batter. Place the raisins one at a time on the top of the batter and gently press them into the dough. Bake for fifty minutes in a slow oven. Cool and then ice and decorate with Hallowe'en figures and then cut into blocks.

FALL MENU

BREAKFAST
Grapes
Cereal and Cream
Fried Butterfish, Creole
Hashed Brown Potatoes   Water-cress
Rolls   Coffee

DINNER
Grape Juice Cocktail
Pot Roast Beef, Spanish
Brown Potatoes   String Beans
Tomato Salad
Rolls   Coffee

SUPPER
Fried Tomatoes   Cream Gravy
Potato Salad
Corn Bread   Apple Sauce
Tea

BUTTERFISH, CREOLE

Cleanse the fish and wash well and then drain. Now roll lightly in flour and brown in hot fat quickly. Place in a baking dish and add the following sauce:

One cup of stewed tomatoes,
Four onions, chopped fine,
One teaspoon of salt,
One teaspoon of paprika,
One-half teaspoon of thyme.

Bake in the oven for twenty minutes and then serve from the dish. Other fish may be used in place of the butter fish.

WINTER MENU

BREAKFAST
Grapes
Cereal and Cream
Virginia Griddle Cakes   Syrup
Coffee

DINNER

Home-made Chow-chow   Piccalilli

Ye Olde-Tyme English Oyster Pye

Mashed Potatoes   Buttered and Spiced Beets

Coleslaw

Grape Tapioca Blanc Mange

Coffee

SUPPER

Bean Sausages   Cream Gravy

Potato Salad

Raisin Cake   Tea

A nice change for the family is to give them corn muffins and plain rolls or biscuits in place of bread. Usually in the hurry and bustle of getting the business folk off in time in the morning and then preparing the children for school the housewife does not have the time to prepare these homey, old-fashioned breads for breakfast.

The price of butter makes it almost prohibitive to use it as a spread for hot cakes, yet we all like the butter flavor. So let us follow the example of the thrifty New England woman, who puts the syrup into a good-sized pitcher and then adds two tablespoons of butter to one and one-half cups of syrup. Place the pitcher into a pan of warm water and then heat. Stir frequently, so that the butter will melt and blend thoroughly with the syrup. Just before sending to the table beat thoroughly. This not only makes a delicious spread for hot cakes and waffles and the like, but it is a real economy and a saving in butter.

GRAPE-JUICE COCKTAIL

Place one pound of grapes in a saucepan and add three cups of water. Bring to a boil and cook until soft. Rub through a fine sieve and then sweeten and chill. Fill into cocktail glasses and serve.

POT ROAST BEEF, SPANISH

Place in a mixing bowl and chop fine

Two tomatoes,
Four onions,
Three green peppers,
Four branches of parsley.

Now add

One teaspoon of paprika.

Mix and pack into the meat, pushing well into the roll. Roll the meat in flour and then melt the suet in a deep saucepan and add the meat. Brown well and add one-half cup of flour. Stir until well browned and then add one quart of boiling water. Cover closely and then cook, allowing one-half hour for each pound of meat, gross weight. One hour before cooking add six small onions and one carrot cut in quarters.

When ready to serve, add one quart of boiling water and season to taste. This will provide sufficient gravy to use for two meals.

GRAPE TAPIOCA BLANC MANGE

Place in a saucepan

One cup of water,
Two cups of grape juice,
Three-quarters cup of finely granulated tapioca.

Bring to a boil and then cook slowly for thirty minutes and then add

Three-quarters cup of sugar,
One-half teaspoon of salt.

Cook five minutes longer. Now rinse custard cups with cold water and pour in the blanc mange. Let cool and then turn on a saucer and pile with the fruit whip made from

White of an egg,
One-half glass of jelly.

Beat until it holds its shape.

BEAN SAUSAGE

Open a can of beans and drain well, then mash and put through a sieve into a mixing bowl. Add

Two onions, grated,
Two tablespoons of parsley, chopped fine,
One-quarter teaspoon of mustard,
One-half teaspoon of paprika.

Mix well and then mould into sausages. Roll them in flour and brown in hot fat. Use the liquid drained from the beans and sufficient milk to measure one and one-half cups. Place in a saucepan and add five tablespoons of flour. Stir to dissolve and then bring to a boil and cook for five minutes. Add

Three-quarters teaspoon of salt,
One-quarter teaspoon of pepper,
Two tablespoons of finely-minced parsley.

VIRGINIA GRIDDLE CAKES

Place one cup of corn meal in a mixing bowl and add

One teaspoon of salt,
Three tablespoons of shortening,
Three tablespoons of syrup,
One cup of boiling water.

Beat to mix and then add

Two cups of cold water,
One egg,

Two and one-half cups of flour,
Two level tablespoons of baking powder.

Beat hard to mix and then bake on a hot griddle.

BUTTERED AND SPICED BEETS

Cook the beets until tender and then drain and cut into slices. Now place in a small saucepan

One tablespoon of butter,
Two tablespoons of vinegar,
Two tablespoons of hot water,
One teaspoon of salt,
One teaspoon of paprika,
One-eighth teaspoon of mustard,
Tiny pinch of cloves.

When boiling hot, pour over the sliced beets.

Use the yolk of egg for making the dressing for the cole slaw and the white of egg and one-half glass of jelly for making the meringue for the grape tapioca blanc mange.

YE OLD-TYME OYSTER PYE

To prepare the crust, place in a mixing bowl

Two cups of sifted flour,
One teaspoon of salt,
Two teaspoons of baking powder.

Sift to mix and then put one-quarter pound of suet through the food-chopper. Then rub the finely chopped suet through a fine sieve to remove the stringy parts. Now rub the suet into the flour and mix to a dough with one-half cup of cold water. Then chop and fold for two minutes. Turn on a floured pastry board and divide into two pieces. Roll out one-half of the dough until one-quarter inch thick and then turn a large plate over this dough and cut around the edge of the plate. Be sure that the plate is at least two inches larger than the top of the baking or casserole dish.

Now drain the oysters and look over carefully for the bits of shell. Place the oysters in a casserole or baking dish and add the stalk of celery that has been scraped clean and then diced and cooked until tender, also

One grated onion,
Three tablespoons of parsley,
Three cups of thick cream sauce,
One and one-half teaspoons of salt,
One teaspoon of white pepper,
One-eighth teaspoon of thyme.

Mix thoroughly and then make two or three small gashes in the top of the crust and cover the oysters with it, pressing the crust well against the edges of the dish. Brush the top of crust with water and bake in a moderate oven for thirty-five minutes.

Use equal parts of the oyster liquor and milk for making the cream sauce. Chop the celery leaves as well as the stalk.

Now roll out the balance of the pastry and cut into three-inch squares. Score the tops lightly with a knife or prick with a fork, and place on a baking sheet and bake a delicate light brown. Wrap in a napkin to keep warm. When ready to serve the oyster pie, place two of the squares of pastry on a plate and then lift on the oyster pie, and then place a second piece right over the crust of pie. Pour over this top piece of pastry two tablespoons of the sauce from the oyster pie.

RAISIN CAKE

Place in a mixing bowl

Three-quarters cup of sugar,
One egg,
Four tablespoons of shortening,
Two cups of flour,

Four teaspoons of baking powder,
Three-quarters cup of water.

Beat to thoroughly mix and then pour into well-greased and floured loaf-shaped pan. Now spread one-half package of raisins on top and gently press them with the back of the spoon until the dough covers them. Bake in a moderate oven for thirty-five minutes.

TURKEY

A creole method of roasting turkey, chicken, duck or game or broiling fowl, birds or game is given below. Clean and prepare the bird to suit the taste, and when ready to cook, whether broiling, roasting or baking, lard the breast with many strips of salt pork or bacon, or fastened on with toothpicks. Place in a hot oven to sear, then turn the bird, be it large or small, on its breast. Roast, bake or broil for three-quarters of the time on its breast, basting every ten minutes. Dredge occasionally with flour. Do not season at the beginning of cooking, but delay this until the last quarter of the time allotted for cooking the bird, then turn it on its breast to brown.

Finish cooking, basting every ten minutes. This method permits the heat to cook the heaviest part of the bird slowly, so that, by turning on its breast, the bony structure may receive the intense heat.

Birds or fowls that are old should be steamed before roasting. This method will make them tender and juicy.

FILLING AND GRAVY

DRY FILLING

One pint of stale bread crumbs,
One large onion, minced fine,
One teaspoon of poultry seasoning,
One teaspoon of salt,
Two tablespoons of bacon fat or good beef drippings.

Rub all together into a crumby mass, then pack into the fowl.

BAKED CHICKEN AND NOODLES

Prepare the chicken for fricasseeing, cook until tender and then lift it. Now cook the noodles in the broth and season. Lift the cooked noodles into a baking or casserole dish. Now brown the chicken quickly on one side in a frying pan, using just sufficient shortening to prevent burning. Lay the chicken on the noodles and then thicken the broth slightly, adding

One tablespoon of minced parsley,
One tablespoon of minced onion.

Pour over the chicken and noodles and bake in a hot oven for twenty-five minutes.

APPLE AND RAISIN FILLING FOR DUCK

Chop enough apples fine to measure one pint. Add

One-half cup of seeded raisins,
One and one-half cups of bread crumbs.

Season with salt, pepper and sweet marjoram. Mix together with two tablespoonsful of melted butter. Pack into duck.

GIBLET GRAVY

Mince the giblets fine. Brown into two tablespoonfuls of bacon fat, adding two tablespoonfuls of flour. Brown well, then add one quart of water. Cook slowly while the fowl is roasting for one and one-half hours. Rub through a sieve, then return to the fire and bring to a boil. It is then ready to serve.

MINCED GIBLETS ON TOAST

Cook the giblets for one hour in one pint of water. Put through the food chopper, adding

One onion,
One hard-boiled egg,
One-fourth cup of canned tomatoes.

Season with

One-eighth teaspoon of mustard, salt and pepper to taste.

Serve on toasted strips of bread for luncheon.

TURKEY MEAT BISCUITS

Prepare the dough as for biscuits. Turn out on a pastry board and pat or roll out one-quarter inch thick. Spread one-half of the dough with the prepared turkey meat. Fold over the balance of the dough, press firmly. Cut with a sharp knife into squares and brush the tops of the biscuits with milk. Bake for twenty minutes in a hot oven.

NOTE.—These biscuits may be prepared the night before and placed in a cold place and baked in the morning.

LEFT-OVER TURKEY

UTILIZING THE LEFT-OVER TURKEY

Remove the meat from the carcass, separating the white from the dark meat. Pick the carcass clean and then break the bones and place in a soup kettle and cover with cold water and add

One-half cup of chopped onions,

One-half cup of diced carrots,
One faggot of soup herbs.

Bring to a boil and cook slowly for two hours. Strain into a bowl and this stock can be used for soups, sauces and gravies.

TURKEY CROQUETTES

One and one-half cups of very thick cream sauce,
One cup of fine bread crumbs,
One and one-half cups of turkey meat,
Three tablespoons of finely minced parsley,
Two tablespoons of grated onions,
Two teaspoons of salt,
One teaspoon of paprika.

Mix thoroughly and then mould into croquettes and dip in beaten egg and then into fine bread crumbs. Fry until golden brown in hot fat.

TURKEY AU GRATIN

Two cups of thick cream sauce,
One and one-half cups of turkey meat,
One tablespoon of grated onion,
Three tablespoons of finely minced parsley,
Two hard-boiled eggs, chopped fine,
One and one-half teaspoons of salt,
One-half teaspoon of pepper.

Mix and then pour in a baking dish. Cover the top with fine bread crumbs and two tablespoonfuls of grated cheese and bake for thirty-five minutes in a moderate oven.

TURKEY, TERRAPIN STYLE

Use the dark meat. Prepare one and one-half cupfuls of cream sauce and then add

One and one-half cups of prepared turkey meat,
Two hard-boiled eggs, cut in eighths,
Pinch of nutmeg,
One teaspoon of salt,
One-half teaspoon of white pepper,
Juice of one lemon.

Heat slowly to boiling point and then add one-half cupful of brown sauce, made from turkey stock. Add one teaspoonful of grated lemon rind and then serve.

MEAT ROLL

Use level measurements. This is a very nice dish for a luncheon. Place in a bowl

Two cups of sifted flour,
One and one-half teaspoons of salt,
One-quarter teaspoon of paprika,
Four teaspoons of baking powder.

Sift twice and then rub in three tablespoonfuls of shortening and then mix to dough with two-thirds cup of water. Roll out on slightly floured board one-quarter inch thick, and spread with finely minced turkey meat, which has been seasoned with

One tablespoon of grated onion,
One green or red pepper, minced fine,
One teaspoon of salt,
One-half teaspoon of paprika.

Roll for jelly-roll and pinch the edges together well. Place in well-greased baking pan and bake for forty-five minutes in a hot oven. Start basting with one cupful of turkey stock after the roll has been in the oven for ten minutes. Serve by cutting in slices and then cover with cream sauce.

TURKEY POT PIE

Place in a baking dish a layer of parboiled and diced potatoes. Season with finely minced onion and parsley and green or red pepper, chopped fine. Now add a layer of turkey meat. Repeat this until the dish is full and then add a sauce made from

One cup of milk,
One cup of turkey stock,
Five tablespoons of flour.

Stir until flour is dissolved in the milk and stock and bring to a boil. Season and then pour over the turkey in the baking dish. Cover the top of the dish with lattice strips of pastry. Brush with milk or water and bake forty-five minutes in a hot oven.

SOME SOUPS USING THE TURKEY STOCK

Made by simmering bones and carcass of turkey in sufficient water to cover.

TURKEY SOUP, ITALIAN

Cook three ounces of macaroni in one quart of boiling water for twenty minutes and then drain and blanch under running water. Place in a saucepan and add

Two and one-half pints of turkey stock,
Two onions, cut fine,
Tiny bit of garlic.

Cook slowly for fifteen minutes and then serve with grated cheese.

MULLIGATAWNEY

Place four cupfuls of turkey stock in a saucepan and add

Three apples, chopped fine.
One carrot,
One small onion.

Bring to a boil and cook slowly until vegetables are soft and then place three tablespoonfuls of shortening in saucepan and add one-half cupful of flour. Stir until well browned and then add two cupfuls of turkey stock. Cook for ten minutes and add to the soup. Bring to a boil, then strain and season with

One level tablespoon of salt,
One and one-half teaspoons of paprika,
One-fourth teaspoon of nutmeg,
Three pints of turkey stock,
One-half cup of finely chopped celery,
One carrot diced,
Four tablespoons of washed rice.

Bring to a boil and cook for thirty-five minutes very slowly and then season.

CABBAGE PUDDING

Chop one medium-sized head of cabbage fine and parboil until tender. Then drain and place in a bowl and add

Two onions, grated,
One cup of left over cold meat, chopped fine.

Season well and then place a layer of the prepared cabbage in a baking dish and then a layer of bread crumbs. Pour two cups of thick cream sauce over all and place a thin layer of bread crumbs on top. Bake in a moderate oven for thirty minutes.

FAMILY THANKSGIVING DINNER FOR SIX PERSONS, FROM A NEW ENGLAND FARM HOUSE

Oyster Soup
Home Pickled Onions
Chow-chow   Chili Sauce
Boston Brown Bread

                    Fish Balls
        Roast Turkey   Brown Gravy
        Oyster Filling   Cranberry Sauce
                    Bannocks
        Baked Potatoes   Mashed Turnips
        Creamed Onions   Buttered Parsnips
                    Coleslaw
            Pepperhash   Corn Relish
            Jams, Jellies and Conserves
    Mince and Pumpkin Pies   Coffee
            Maple Fudge   Preserved Plums

The good old-fashioned oyster soup, made from the famous recipe that has been in the family for so many years, was served from two immense old white china tureens. Grandpa Perkins, sitting at the head of the table, ladled out the soup, and after it was placed and every one was seated, grandpa rapped the table with the big horn handle of the carving knife and every head was bowed in silent prayer while his voice was uplifted in thankful Thanksgiving praise, to which we all responded with a solemn amen.

CHICKEN ROLL

Place in a mixing bowl

Three cups of sifted flour.
One teaspoon of salt,
Three level tablespoons of baking powder.

Sift to mix, rub in five tablespoons of shortening and mix to dough with one cup of water. Roll on pastry board one-quarter inch thick and spread with the prepared filling. Roll as for jelly-roll, place in well-greased and floured baking pan and bake in a moderate oven for thirty-five minutes. Serve with tomato or creole sauce.

PREPARED FILLING

Mince the giblets fine and pick the meat from the neck and carcass, putting the skin through the food-chopper. Place in a bowl and add

Two onions, grated,
One green pepper, minced fine,
Four tablespoons of finely-chopped parsley,
One-half cup of bacon, cut in dice and nicely browned,
One teaspoon of salt,
One-half teaspoon of white pepper.

Mix thoroughly and spread as directed upon the dough.

BOSTON BROWN BREAD

Place in a mixing bowl

One-half cup of cornmeal,
One-half cup of barley flour,
One-half cup of rice flour,
One teaspoon of salt,
One-half cup of molasses,
One level teaspoon of soda,
One and one-quarter cups of sour milk.

Beat to mix and then pour into well-greased one-pound empty coffee cans and fill them three-quarters full. Cover and place in a deep saucepan. Fill the saucepan two-thirds full of boiling water. Boil steadily for one and three-quarters hours; then remove the lid from coffee can and place in a warm oven for three-quarters of an hour to dry out.

Next come the fish balls—not the great, round old-fashioned grease-soaked one of commerce, but the daintiest golden brown balls the size of bantam eggs, fried in smoking hot fat and laid on snowy white napkins in piles, with sprigs of parsley stuck between them.

AUNT POLLY RIVES'S ONE-EGG CAKE

One egg,

One cup of brown sugar,
Five tablespoons of shortening,

Cream well and then add

One and three-quarter cups of flour,
Four teaspoons of baking powder,
One cup of milk.

Beat to thoroughly mix. Add one cup of seeded raisins; pour in a well-greased and floured loaf-shaped pan and bake forty minutes in moderate oven.

REAL OLD VERMONT OYSTER SOUP

For six people.

Drain one dozen oysters free from the liquid, then strain the liquid into a saucepan. Wash and look carefully over the oysters to remove all bits of shell. Chop the oysters very fine and then return them to the oyster liquid. Add one tablespoon of butter and a tiny pinch of thyme; then heat to the scalding point and add two and one-half cups of scalding hot milk. Let come to a boil, remove from the fire and serve. Scald the milk in a double boiler.

COUSIN HETTY'S FISH BALLS

"Time was," said Cousin Hetty, "when we used to flake out fish, but since brother and old Amos went into the fish business, we generally use the shredded fish."

Recipe for six persons. Open a package of prepared shredded codfish and then turn into a piece of cheese-cloth and plunge four or five times into a large bowl of hot water. Squeeze dry. Cook and then mash sufficient potatoes to measure three cups and then add the prepared fish and

Two tablespoons of grated onion,
Four tablespoons of finely-minced parsley,

One teaspoon of paprika,
One-quarter cup of milk,
Two tablespoons of butter.

Beat hard to mix thoroughly and then mould into small balls; roll in flour; dip in beaten egg and milk and then roll in fine crumbs and fry until golden brown in hot fat.

BANNOCKS

For six persons. Place in a saucepan

Two cups of boiling water,
One-half teaspoon of salt,
Two tablespoons of maple sugar,
Four tablespoons of syrup,
Three-quarters cup of cornmeal.

Cook until it is a thick cornmeal mush, then let cool. Spread very thin on well-greased baking sheet; brush with melted shortening and bake in a hot oven. In the days of long ago these bannocks were usually baked before the open fire.

The feature of the dinner, three large turkeys, were cooked until golden brown and juicy tender. Nigh about the coming of the first of October, grandma gives strict orders that every morsel of bread crumbs, even though it is just the war bread, be saved. For you know lots of bread crumbs are needed for the fish cakes and then filling of the birds. This stale bread is thoroughly dried out and then put through the food chopper, then sifted. The coarse crumbs are used for filling the turkey.

In the good old days of yesteryear when a large majority of us felt that Thanksgiving would be incomplete without the turkey, it required careful planning to use the left-overs without waste, as the family quickly tired of too much turkey when served for three or four meals.

However, left-over chicken or turkey may be served in the following dishes:

BROWN EMINCE FOWL

Pick the meat from the back, carcass and neck and mince fine the giblets. Place in a saucepan and add to one and one-half cups of the prepared meat

One onion,
One green pepper, minced fine,
Three-quarters cup of boiling water.

Cook gently for twenty-five minutes, then place in a saucepan two tablespoons of shortening and four tablespoons of flour. Stir to blend thoroughly and then brown until a rich golden brown. Turn in the prepared emince and stir to mix and season with

Salt,
White pepper,
Tiny pinch of mustard,
Tiny pinch of poultry seasoning.

Make a border of mashed potatoes on a warm platter and fill the emince in the centre of the platter and garnish with finely minced parsley.

CHICKEN DUMPLINGS

Remove all the meat from the left-over carcass and break the bones. Place the bones in a stock pot and add

Three pints of cold water,
Two onions,
One faggot of potherbs,
One cup of well-crushed tomatoes.

Bring to a boil and simmer slowly for two and one-half hours. Strain the stock and season with

Salt,
White pepper,
Three tablespoons of finely-minced parsley.

Now place sufficient meat picked from the carcass through the food chopped to measure, when chopped fine, one cup; place in a bowl and add

One large onion, grated,
Four tablespoons of finely-chopped minced parsley,
One teaspoon of salt,
One-half teaspoon of white pepper,
Two cups of sifted flour,
Three level teaspoons of baking powder,
One tablespoon of shortening,
One well-beaten egg,
Seven tablespoons of water.

Work to a smooth dough, then drop from the tablespoon into boiling stock. Cover closely and let cook for fifteen minutes. Lift on a slice of toast and then quickly add to the stock

One cup of minced chicken.

Then dissolve

One-half cup of flour,
One-half cup of water,

and stir to blend thoroughly. Add to the stock and then bring to a boil; cook for five minutes and pour over the dumplings. Sprinkle with finely minced parsley and send to the table at once.

CHICKEN LOAF

This delightful old southern dish is always welcomed by the family. Put the meat picked from the carcass and neck, with the giblets, through the food chopper, about one and one-half cups. Mince fine one-half cup of bacon and sufficient onions to measure one cup. Brown the bacon and simmer the onions in the bacon fat until tender, taking care not to brown. Now add

Two and one-half cups of cold cooked rice,
One cup of very thick cream sauce,

One cup of fine bread crumbs,
One tablespoon of Worcestershire sauce,
One and one-half teaspoons of salt,
One teaspoon of white pepper,
One well-beaten egg.

Mix thoroughly, then pack into well-greased and floured loaf-shaped pan. Set the pan in a large one containing warm water and bake for one hour in a slow oven. Remove the pan containing the water and let the loaf stay in the moderate oven for fifteen minutes. Serve with parsley, cream or tomato sauce while hot; cut the balance cold and serve with mayonnaise or tartare sauce.

CHRISTMAS DINNER

Clear Tomato Soup

Onion Relish   Curly Celery

Baked Chicken

Spicy Filling   Brown Gravy

Cranberry Jelly

Sweet Potato Pone   Mashed Turnips

Coleslaw

Mince Pie   Coffee

ONION RELISH

Chop fine sufficient onions to measure one cup and then place two tablespoons of fat in a frying pan. When hot, add the onions, cover closely and simmer slowly until tender. Season with salt and paprika and three tablespoons of vinegar. Cool and serve as a relish.

CURLY CELERY

Scrape and thoroughly cleanse two stalks of celery and remove part of the green top and the bruised outside pieces. Cut each stalk in half from the root to the stem and then split again. Place in cold water and allow to crisp and cool.

GRANDMA PERKINS'S SPICY FILLING

Put the green and rough outside parts of the celery

Four onions,
One bunch of potherbs,

through the food chopper and chop fine; then add

Three cups of stale bread crumbs,
One and one-half teaspoons of salt,
Five tablespoons of shortening,
One teaspoon of pepper,
Three-quarters cup of chicken stock.

Mix and then fill into the prepared chicken. Sew the opening with a stout darning needle and string. Now rub the chicken thoroughly with shortening and cover with flour. Place in the oven and let brown slightly; then turn the chicken breast down and baste every ten minutes. Turning the chicken with the breast down causes the juices to permeate the white meat and thus make it tender and juicy.

Turn the chicken and allow the breast about twenty minutes for browning before taking from the oven.

BAKED CHICKEN

Select a plump stewing chicken about five pounds and then singe, draw and wash thoroughly. Cover slowly and steam until tender; then fill with a spicy filling and place in a moderate oven to roast for one and three-quarters hours, basting every ten minutes.

In order to be sure that the fowl will be sufficiently tender, remember to steam it ahead of time.

CRANBERRY JELLY

Wash one pint of cranberries; then drain and place in a saucepan. Add three-quarters cup of water. Cover and cook until soft; then rub through a fine sieve. Add two cups of brown sugar and bring to a boil. Cook for ten minutes and then pour into small custard cups to mould.

SWEET POTATO PONE

Wash and then boil one-quarter peck of sweet potatoes. Cool and remove the skins. Place in a bowl and mash, seasoning with

One-half teaspoon of nutmeg,
One and one-half teaspoons of salt,
One-half teaspoon of pepper,
Two tablespoons of butter.

Grease a baking pan well; then dust with flour and spread the prepared sweet potatoes in the pan about one inch thick. Sprinkle the top thickly with nutmeg and place one tablespoon of butter over the top in tiny dots. Bake in a moderate oven for twenty-five minutes. Remove from the oven and let stand for five minutes. Cut into squares and lift with a cake turner to a hot plate.

COLESLAW

Shred the cabbage fine and then chop one green pepper. Place in water to crisp. Make a mayonnaise dressing by placing on a plate

Yolk of one egg,
One teaspoon of mustard,
One-half teaspoon of paprika,
One teaspoon of sugar,
One teaspoon of vinegar.

Work to a smooth paste and then add the oil slowly at first and then faster until all the oil is thoroughly incorporated, beating it quite hard. Add the salt to taste. Now add the vinegar to reduce to desired consistency; then drain the cabbage, turn on a cloth and let dry before pouring over the dressing. Use three-quarters cup salad oil.

MINCE PIE

Two cups of flour,
One-half teaspoon of salt,
One teaspoon of baking powder,
Two teaspoons of sugar.

Place in a mixing bowl and then sift. Now rub three-quarters cup of shortening and mix to a dough with about six tablespoons of water. Divide the dough, then roll out and cover a pie plate. Use one and one-half pounds of mincemeat to fill. Cover with a crust and then wash with beaten egg. Bake in a moderate oven for forty-five minutes.

NOTE.—To wash the pie use one-half of beaten egg, using the balance in the chicken filling.

You know there is a great little story told about the pie-loving New Englanders, and as the story goes, there are only two kinds of pie, namely, "'Tis mince and 'tain't mince." So, as Grandma Perkins says, "This is all mince."

HOW TO PREPARE THE MINCE

Twelve medium-sized apples,
One-half pound of candied citron,
One-half package of seeded raisins,
One pound of shelled peanuts,
Three-quarters pound of suet,
One pound of dried peaches,
One lemon.

Put all through the food chopper and then place

One quart of syrup,
One pound of brown sugar,

in a preserving kettle and bring to a boil. Cook for ten minutes and then add the prepared fruits and suet that have been put through the food chopper and add

One package of seeded raisins,
One tablespoon of cinnamon,
One teaspoon of ginger,
One teaspoon of cloves,
One-half teaspoon of allspice,
One-half teaspoon of nutmeg,
One-half teaspoon of salt,
Three-quarters cup of strong cider vinegar.

Stir to mix thoroughly, then cook for ten minutes. Cool and then fill into fruit jars. Pour one tablespoon of salad oil on top; adjust the rubber and lid and seal. Process in hot water bath for twenty minutes and then cool and store.

This mince will be found to be most delicious, and it will keep until used. Grandma Perkins's grandad was a Hiram Teesdale, of Gloucester, England, and this recipe is over 400 years old. The original recipe was named Christmas Mynce Pye, and on the holidays, a great pye of Gloucester mynce, made by good dame Teesdale, was always sent as a tithe from the county to the good Queene Elizabeth, and in this way royal favor was conferred on this family by the queen, who was delighted with the wonderful concoction.

Black walnuts and hazel nuts were used in the original recipe, but as these nuts are quite expensive, the peanuts will do just as well.

CHRISTMAS GOODIES

In the days of long ago, before the day of heated apartments and water-heated homes, the housewife used the cellar as the cold-storage room. To-day this is impossible. For the householder who has an outside enclosed laundry or summer kitchen, the problem of keeping the holiday delicacies is quite an easy one. But to those of us who dwell in flats and apartments, some other way must be arranged.

Here are two new ideas that are worth trying: First, a window box on the shady side of the house. This box must be lined with asbestos paper on the inside, and then covered with the same paper and an additional covering of oil cloth upon the outside.

By covering the box in this way, the housewife is assured of a smaller storage space of an even temperature. Neither the extreme cold nor heat will affect this box. A thick layer of newspapers may be used as a lining, between the inside covering of the asbestos and the oil cloth covering upon the outside of the box.

Mincemeat must be stored in a cool, dry place to blend and ripen, without the danger of freezing. This is also an ideal time for the mother to plan to have the family help her and at the same time knit the home ties very closely together. The home where the family joins in the evening to make the seasonable delicacies is a very happy one. Let the children have some of their friends in to help them with the preparations.

CHICKEN CUSTARD

Place one pint of chicken stock in a mixing bowl and add

One small onion, grated,
One and one-half teaspoons of salt,
One-half teaspoon of paprika,
Four eggs.

Beat until thoroughly mixed and then fill into well-buttered glass custard cups and set the cups in a baking pan and fill the pan half full of warm water. Place in a slow oven to bake until firm. Remove from the oven and let stand for five minutes to settle, then loosen the edges of the custard from the cups with a knife and turn on a slice of toast and serve with parsley sauce. This is a delicious luncheon dish.

MEATLESS MINCEMEAT

Place in a mixing bowl

Four pounds of apples, chopped fine,
One pound of peanuts, chopped fine,
One pound of dried apricots, chopped fine,
One pound of dried peaches, chopped fine,
One pound of suet, chopped fine,
Two packages of seeded raisins,
One package of currants,
One-quarter pound of candied citron, chopped fine,
One-quarter pound of candied orange peel, chopped fine,
One-quarter pound of candied lemon peel, chopped fine,
Two tablespoons of cinnamon,
One teaspoon of mace,
One teaspoon of ginger,
One teaspoon of allspice,
One teaspoon of cloves,
One teaspoon of salt,
One pint jar of grape or other preserves,
One quart of molasses,
One quart of cider, boiled for fifteen minutes.

Mix thoroughly and then store in the same manner as for ye olde-tyme mincemeat.

YE OLDE-TYME MINCEMEAT

Purchase one pound of shin beef and one-half pound of good soup bones, preferably bones from the chine or rib. Wipe the meat, place it and the bones in a saucepan and add three cups of boiling water. Cook slowly without seasoning until the meat is tender. Cool and then pick the meat from the bones and put all the meat through the food chopper into a large bowl and add

One pound of suet, shredded fine,
Five pounds of apples, chopped fine,
Grated rind of three lemons,
Juice of three lemons,
One-half pound of candied orange peel, shredded fine,

One-half pound of lemon peel, shredded fine,
One-half pound of citron peel, shredded fine,
One pound of dried or evaporated peaches, shredded fine,
One pound of shelled peanuts, chopped fine,
Two packages of seeded raisins,
One package of currants,
Three level tablespoons of cinnamon,
Two level teaspoons of mace,
Two level teaspoons of allspice,
One level teaspoon of cloves,
One level teaspoon of ginger,
Two level teaspoons of salt.

Mix thoroughly, then place in a deep saucepan

One quart of syrup,
One pound of brown sugar,
One and one-half cups of stock from the meat,
One quart of cider,
One-quarter cup of vinegar.

Bring to a boil and cook for twenty minutes. Pour over the mincemeat and mix thoroughly. Fill into crocks or jars; cover closely and set in a cool place, or fill it into all-glass jars and adjust the rubber and lid. Seal and then place in a hot-water bath. Process for one-half hour, at a temperature of 185 degrees Fahrenheit. Remove and store in a cool place. Mincemeat that has been sterilized will keep until used.

GREEN TOMATO MINCE

Place one quart of thinly sliced green tomatoes in a bowl and sprinkle with four tablespoons of salt. Let stand for four hours, then drain and squeeze dry. Return to the bowl and add

One-half pound of finely chopped suet,
Two and one-half pounds of finely chopped apples,
One cup of finely chopped dried apricots,
One cup of finely chopped seeded raisins,

One cup of finely chopped peanuts,
One cup of plum preserves,
Two cups of molasses,
One and one-half cups of boiled cider,
One tablespoon of cinnamon,
One-half teaspoon of nutmeg,
One-half teaspoon of cloves,
One-quarter teaspoon of allspice,
One-half teaspoon of ginger.

Mix thoroughly and then store in the same manner as for ye olde-time mincemeat.

MINCEMEAT FOR TWO

One-half cup of finely chopped cold cooked meat,
Three-quarters cup of finely chopped suet,
Six cups of finely chopped apples,
One cup of finely chopped candied orange and lemon peel, mixed,
One cup of seeded raisins,
One cup of currants,
One cup of chopped peanuts,
One cup of chopped apricots,
One and one-half cups of molasses,
One cup of cider,
Four tablespoons of vinegar,
One tablespoon of cinnamon,
One teaspoon of nutmeg,
One teaspoon of allspice,
One-half teaspoon of ginger,
One-half teaspoon of salt.

Mix and then store in the same manner as for ye old-tyme mincemeat.

JEWISH OR KOSHER MINCEMEAT

Chop fine sufficient left-over cold cooked beef or lamb free from all fat to measure two cups. Place in a large bowl and add

Two quarts of finely chopped apples,
One cup of finely chopped candied orange peel,
One cup of finely chopped candied lemon peel,
One cup of finely chopped citron,
One cup of finely chopped apricots,
Two cups each of seedless raisins and currants,
One cup of finely chopped shelled almonds,
One cup of corn oil,
One and one-half tablespoons of cinnamon,
One teaspoon of cloves,
One teaspoon of nutmeg,
One teaspoon of allspice,
One-half teaspoon of ginger,
One teaspoon of salt.

Now place in a saucepan

One quart of cider.
One pound of brown sugar,
One cup of molasses.

Stir to dissolve, then bring to a boil and cook for fifteen minutes. Pour over the mincemeat and mix thoroughly. Fill into crocks or jars and store as for ye olde-tyme mincemeat.

When storing mincemeat either in crocks or in jars, cover with salad oil, about one-quarter inch deep, to exclude air. Use a good grade of salad oil. This makes it unnecessary to use liquor for keeping the mincemeat.

The bride housewife who is planning a Thanksgiving dinner for "just us two" frequently finds herself in a dilemma. Turkey is much too large for her and chicken hardly appeals to her for this day. However, below are some suggestive menus for a Thanksgiving dinner for two.

No. 1.

Celery Radishes
Oysters on the Half Shell
Planked Squab Spiced Grape Jam
Baked Sweet Potatoes
Creamed Onions
Endive Salad Russian Dressing
Individual Mince Tarts
Coffee
Cheese and Crackers Nuts and Raisins

No. 2.
Grilled Oysters
Celery
Fillets of Flounder, Piedmont
Guinea Hen, Marie Cranberry Jelly
Candied Sweet Potatoes Cauliflower
Coleslaw
Pumpkin Tarts Coffee
Cheese Nuts and Raisins

No. 3.
Shrimp Cocktail
Celery Olives
Roast Squab Duckling, Currant Jelly
Creamed Mashed Potatoes Peas
Lettuce Pimento Dressing
Mince Turnover Coffee
Cheese and Crackers
Nuts and Raisins

HOW TO PREPARE THE MENU

Place the oysters in the ice box, near the ice, until ready to serve. Scrape and clean the celery, cutting the root into a point, then splitting it in half from root end to tip.

Place in cold water and trim, then cleanse the radishes. Split the radishes into four parts, from tip to near the stem end; use a sharp knife for this purpose—this makes eight cuts in the radishes. Place in cold water.

Wash the oyster shells and set aside until needed for serving the oysters.

PLANKED SQUAB

Split the squab down the back, then draw. Wash well in cold water and remove the breast bone. Place in a baking pan, rub with shortening and dust very lightly with the flour. Place in a hot oven to bake for thirty-five minutes. Baste frequently with hot water. Now lift to a hot plank and cover with strips of bacon. Split the sweet potatoes and place on each corner. Brush lightly with butter, dust with cinnamon and brown sugar. Place in a hot oven for twelve minutes.

GUINEA HEN MARIE

Have the butcher split the hen down the back and remove the breast bone. Wash and wipe dry, then rub well with shortening and dust with flour. Lay in a baking pan and place in a hot oven. Baste every ten minutes with boiling water. Cook for forty minutes in a moderate oven and just ten minutes before removing from the oven cover the hen with strips of bacon and

Three onions, minced fine,
One green pepper, minced fine,

GRILLED OYSTERS

Carefully look over the oyster and remove all bits of shell. Wash and then roll in mayonnaise, dip in bread crumbs. Return to the deep shell and broil or bake in a hot oven for ten minutes.

PASTRY FOR TWO

Place in a mixing bowl

One cup of flour,
One teaspoon of baking powder,
One-half teaspoon of salt.

Sift to mix, then rub in three tablespoons of shortening and mix to a dough with three tablespoons of water. Chop the water into the flour, then turn on the pastry board and roll out one-quarter inch thick. Use for tarts and turnovers. Brush with milk or syrup and water and bake in a moderate oven.

CAKE FOR TWO

Place in a mixing bowl

Three-quarters cup of white corn syrup,
Yolk of one egg,
Four tablespoons of water,
One cup of sifted flour,
Three level teaspoons of baking powder,
One level teaspoon of flavoring.

BUFFET SUPPER

No. 1
Salted Nuts   Celery
Tuna Fish à la King
Asparagus Salad   Russian Dressing
Ice Cream   Cake
Coffee

No. 2
Olives   Pickles
Chicken Salad   Apple Jelly
Rice Croquettes
Ice Cream   Cake   Coffee

No. 3
Olives   Radishes
Baked Ham Sandwiches
Potato and Celery Salad
Ice Cream   Cake   Coffee

FOR MENU NO. 1

Materials required:

Pound of almonds,
Six stalks of celery,
Eight large cans of tuna fish,

One can of pimentos,
One-half pound of mushrooms,
Six quarts of milk,
Three large cans of asparagus,
Six quarts of ice cream, cut five blocks to the quart,
Eight-pound wedding cake,
One pound of coffee,
One pound of sugar,
One can of milk,
Twenty-five rolls,
One pound of butter.

TUNA FISH A LA KING

Open cans of fish and turn into a large bowl. Make the sauce as follows. Place in a saucepan

Six quarts of milk,
Five level cups of flour.

Stir to blend thoroughly, then bring to a boil and cook slowly for five minutes. Now add

One can of chopped pimentos,
The prepared mushrooms,
Three level tablespoons of salt,
Two level tablespoons of paprika,
One teaspoon of pepper.

The tuna fish should be broken in large pieces. Heat slowly and when hot serve on thin slices of toast.

TO PREPARE THE MUSHROOMS

Peel the mushrooms and then cut both caps and stems in small pieces. Parboil for five minutes in boiling water and then drain and use.

A heart shape may be arranged for either the square or round table. Have the shape made by a carpenter, fastening small cleats underneath to prevent its slipping off table top. The cleats must be arranged so they will catch the edge of the table.

SUPPERS FOR EVENING AFFAIR

                Toasted Cheese Sandwiches
                Gingerbread   Tea
            Cheese and Pepper Sandwiches or
                Bacon and Onion Sandwich
                         Tea

                     Scotch Rabbit
                  Bread and Butter
                        Tea

                    Dry Oyster Pan
              Toast   Cocoa
           Cheese and Omelet Sandwiches
                        Tea

TOASTED CHEESE SANDWICHES

Remove the crust from a loaf of bread, and then cut into slices one inch thick. Toast and then cut American cheese in slices one-fourth inch thick. Place on toast and spread lightly with grated onion. Place in the pan in a hot oven to toast the cheese.

GINGERBREAD

This cake can be made and baked in forty-five minutes. Place in a bowl

One and one-half cups of molasses,
One-half cup of shortening,
One cup of water,

Four cups of sifted flour,
Three level tablespoons of baking powder,
One and one-half teaspoons of cinnamon,
One teaspoon of nutmeg,
One teaspoon of ginger,
One-half teaspoon of allspice,
One-quarter teaspoon of cloves.

Beat just enough to mix and then pour into well-greased and floured pan and bake for forty minutes in a moderate oven. It can be cut and eaten while hot if desired.

CHEESE AND PEPPER SANDWICHES

Place in a bowl

One cup of cottage cheese,
One onion, minced fine,
Two peppers, chopped fine,
One-half cup of mayonnaise,
One teaspoon of salt,
One teaspoon of paprika.

Beat to mix and then butter the bread and cut in thin slices. Place a layer of cheese mixture and then cover and cut in half.

BACON AND ONION SANDWICHES

Mince fine one and one-half cups of onions. Parboil until tender and then mince four ounces of bacon. Cut in dice. Toss lightly in hot pan and add the onions. Toss until onions are nicely browned and tender. Spread between slices of buttered rye bread.

FILLET OF BEEF A LA RIGA

Round skirt, flank or chuck steaks may be used for this dish. Cut one and one-quarter pounds of thin round steak into four pieces. Now mince very fine

Two ounces of salt pork,
Two onions,
Four branches of parsley.

Add

One and one-half cups of prepared bread,
Two teaspoons of salt,
One teaspoon of paprika,
One teaspoon of Worcestershire sauce.

Mix thoroughly and then form into a sausage and lay on the prepared steak and roll, tying securely in three places with white string. Roll the steak in flour and then place four tablespoons of shortening in a deep saucepan and add the prepared fillets, and brown well. When the fillets are nicely browned, stir in two tablespoons of flour well and add

Two cups of boiling water,
One carrot, cut in quarters,
Four small onions.

Cover closely and cook for one hour and then add

Two teaspoons of salt,
One-half teaspoon of pepper,
Juice of one-half lemon,
One cup of peas.

Heat to the boiling point and then cook for ten minutes. Now lay a slice of toast for each fillet on a hot platter and lift the fillet. Remove the strings, then lift the carrot and onions and lay on a platter. Strain over the gravy and then place the peas in a border around the platter, and garnish with thin slices of tomato.

SCOTCH RABBIT

Place one-half pound of grated cheese in a saucepan or chafing dish and add

One onion, grated,
Three-quarters cup of well-drained canned tomatoes,
One tablespoon of Worcestershire sauce,
One well-beaten egg,
One teaspoon of salt,
One teaspoon of paprika.

Mix and heat until the cheese melts. Serve on the toast.

DRY OYSTER PAN

Allow one-half dozen oysters for each person. Look over the oysters carefully and wash to remove bits of shell. Place well-drained oysters in a saucepan and place on stove. Shake continually until cooked, usually about four or five minutes. Season with salt, pepper and one tablespoon of Worcestershire sauce. Lift on a thick slice of toast and pour one tablespoon of melted butter over the oysters and then divide the liquid in the pan and pour over the toast. Sprinkle with finely chopped parsley and serve.

RICE MUFFINS

Rub one cup of cold boiled rice through a fine sieve into a mixing bowl and add

One egg,
One cup of milk,
One teaspoon of salt,
Four tablespoons of syrup,
Three tablespoons of shortening,
One and three-quarters cups of flour,
Four teaspoons of baking powder.

Beat hard to mix and then pour into well-greased and floured muffin pans, and bake in a hot oven for twenty minutes.

SPANISH BUN

One and one-half cups of sugar,

Three-quarters cup of shortening,
Yolks of five eggs.

Cream until light lemon color and then add

Three teaspoons of baking powder,
Five cups of flour,
One cup of milk,
One package of small seedless raisins or currants,
One-half teaspoon of salt.

Beat just enough to mix and then cut and fold in the stiffly beaten whites of five eggs. Pour into square pan which has been lined with paper and then greased and floured. Bake in a moderate oven for one hour. Ice with water-icing and mark off into slices with a knife while the icing is soft.

VEGETABLES A LA JARDINIERE

Pare and cut in dice

Two carrots,
One cup of celery,
One cup of sliced onions.

Place in a saucepan, cover with boiling water and cook until tender; then drain, and then mince fine three slices of bacon. Brown bacon and then lift and add the vegetables to the fat left from browning the bacon. Add

One cup of canned peas,
One and one-half teaspoons of salt,
One teaspoon of paprika,
One tablespoon of vinegar.

Cook slowly for fifteen minutes.

BRAISED OX TAILS

The large ox tail joints or the usual ox tail may be used for this. Soak two and one-half pounds of tails in warm water for fifteen minutes and then wash well, and drain and wipe dry. Roll in flour and then brown quickly in hot fat. Now lift to a deep saucepan and add

Three cups of boiling water,
Two cups of sliced onions,
Two carrots, cut in dice.

Cook slowly for one and one-quarter hours and then season with

Two teaspoons of salt,
One teaspoon of pepper,
Four tablespoons of finely chopped parsley.

Now to serve cook three-quarters pound of macaroni in boiling water for twenty minutes and then drain and season, and place on a hot platter. Lay on top of the macaroni the cooked ox tails and pour over all the gravy containing the onions and carrots. Garnish with finely chopped parsley and serve.

POTATO PANCAKES

Place in a mixing bowl three slices of bacon, minced fine, and cooked until nicely browned

Three tablespoons of bacon fat,
One egg,
Three-quarters cup of milk,
One and one-half cups of flour,
Three-quarters cup of potatoes rubbed through a fine sieve,
Four teaspoons of baking powder.

Beat hard to thoroughly mix and then bake on a griddle or fry in hot fat.

BANANAS A LA JAMIQUE

Peel three bananas and then cut in half. Place in a bowl and sprinkle with the juice of one lemon. Let stand for one hour to marinate, and then dip in a batter and fry until golden brown. Lay on a thin slice of sponge cake and spread the cake with pineapple jelly or jam. Pile high with fruit whip and garnish with finely chopped crystallized ginger.

BOSTON BAKED BEANS

Soak one pint of beans in plenty of cold water overnight and in the morning carefully wash and place in a saucepan and cover again with water. Bring to a boil and cook for ten minutes, and then drain and place in a casserole or baking dish, and add

One-half pound of salt pork, cut into two-inch blocks,
One cup of stewed tomatoes rubbed through a sieve,
Four tablespoons of molasses,
One teaspoon of salt,
One onion, chopped fine,
One-half teaspoon of pepper,
One-quarter teaspoon of mustard.

Mix well and then add sufficient water to cover. Bake in a moderate oven for three hours.

WHOLE WHEAT MUFFINS

Place in a mixing bowl

Two cups of buttermilk,
One teaspoon of baking soda,
One teaspoon of salt,
Three tablespoons of sugar,
Four tablespoons of shortening,
One egg,
Three cups of whole-wheat flour,
Two teaspoons of baking powder.

Beat hard to mix and then pour into well-greased muffin pans and bake for twenty minutes in a hot oven.

YESTERDAY'S BRAN BREAD

Place in a mixing bowl

Three cups of buttermilk,
One and one-half teaspoons of salt,
Two teaspoons of baking soda,
Three-quarters cup of syrup,
One-half cup of shortening.

Beat to thoroughly mix and then add

Four cups of whole-wheat flour,
Three cups of bran,
One and one-half cups of white flour,
Two teaspoons of baking powder.

Beat hard to mix and then pour into two well-greased and floured loaf-shaped pans and spread evenly. Let stand for ten minutes and then bake in a moderate oven for forty minutes. One-half package of seeded raisins or three-quarters cup of finely chopped nuts may be added to one loaf for variety. Use when one day old.

BUTTERMILK CUSTARD

Place in a mixing bowl

Yolk of one egg,
Two eggs,
One and one-quarter cups of buttermilk,
One teaspoon of vanilla extract,
One-half cup of sugar,
Three tablespoons of flour.

Beat to a smooth batter and then pour in custard cups and set the cups in a pan of warm water, and bake in a slow oven until firm in the centre. Remove, cool and then make a whip with

White of one egg,
One-half glass of jelly.

Beat to a stiff meringue and then pile high on each custard. Serve ice cold, dusted with cinnamon.

YANKEE PANCAKES

Place in a mixing bowl

One and one-half cups of buttermilk,
Two tablespoons of syrup,
One tablespoon of shortening,
One teaspoon of baking soda,
One teaspoon of salt.

Beat to mix and then add

One cup of whole-wheat flour,
One-half cup of cornmeal,
One teaspoon of baking powder.

Beat to mix and then bake on a hot gridle.

BUTTERMILK BREAD

Scald two cups of buttermilk and then let cool. Put through a sieve to break up the large curds and then turn into a mixing bowl and add

Four tablespoons of sugar,
One tablespoon of salt,
Four tablespoons of shortening,
One yeast cake dissolved in one-half cup of water.

Beat hard to mix and then add eight cups of flour, and work to a smooth dough; grease the bowl and place the dough in it. Turn the dough over to thoroughly coat with the shortening. Cover and let rise overnight and then early in the morning punch down well and turn over for one hour. Place on a moulding board and divide into loaves. Form into the loaf and then place in well-greased pans and let rise for one hour. Bake in a moderate oven for forty minutes.

It is important that the temperature of the scalded and cooled buttermilk should be about 70 degrees Fahrenheit. When setting the bread overnight, be sure that it is in a place where the average temperature will be 65 degrees Fahrenheit in summer and 70 degrees Fahrenheit in winter, and which is free from drafts.

BUTTERMILK DOUGHNUTS

Place in a mixing bowl

One cup of buttermilk,
Two tablespoons of shortening,
One egg,
One cup of sugar,
One teaspoon of baking soda,
One teaspoon of nutmeg,
One-half teaspoon of ginger.

Beat to mix. Now add

Five cups of sifted flour,
Two teaspoons of baking powder,

and work to a smooth dough. Roll out one-half inch thick on well-floured pastry board and cut and fry until golden brown in hot fat.

BUTTERMILK CHEESE PIE

Place one quart of buttermilk in a pan and heat gently to about 110 degrees Fahrenheit. Let cool and then turn into a piece of cheese-cloth and let drain for two hours. Now measure one and one-half cups of whey and place in a saucepan and add six tablespoons of cornstarch. Stir to dissolve and then bring to a boil and cook for five minutes. Now add

One cup of sugar,
Yolks of two eggs,
Grated rind of one-half lemon,
One teaspoon of nutmeg,
One-half teaspoon of vanilla.

And the prepared cheese that has been draining in the cheesecloth. Beat very hard with the egg-beater to thoroughly blend. Pour into pans which have been lined with plain pastry and bake for forty-five minutes in a moderate oven.

Dust the top of the pie before placing in the oven with either nutmeg or cinnamon, and one-half cup of seeded raisins or finely chopped nuts may be added for variety, if desired.

Use left-over whites of egg

One for fruit whip;
One for dipping croquettes, oysters and the like to be fried in deep fat.

SAUCES

CIDER SAUCE (CHAMPAGNE SAUCE)

Melt three tablespoons of ham fat in the frying pan and add four tablespoons of flour, and cook until nice and brown, then add two cups of cider. Stir until well blended and then bring to a boil. Cook slowly for five minutes and then season with salt and white pepper and a little nutmeg.

MOCK HOLLANDAISE

To one cupful of cream sauce add

Yolk of one egg,

Two tablespoons of lemon juice,
One teaspoon of salt,
One teaspoon of paprika,
One teaspoon of grated onion.

BATARDI SAUCE

One cup of thick cream sauce,

Yolk of one egg,
One teaspoon of paprika,
One teaspoon of salt,
One teaspoon of grated onion,
Juice of one-half lemon,
One-half cup of stewed tomatoes,
One tablespoon of finely minced parsley.

Heat slowly, beating thoroughly to blend. Rub through fine sieve and then serve cold.

TOMATO SAUCE

One cup of canned tomatoes rubbed through a sieve,
One and one-half cups of cold water,
Four onions, minced fine,
One carrot, cut fine,
One faggot of soup herbs.

Cook slowly for twenty minutes and then add

Three tablespoons of cornstarch,
One tablespoon of sugar,
Two teaspoons of salt,
One teaspoon of pepper,
One-quarter teaspoon of mustard dissolved in one-half cup of cold water.

Bring to a boil and then cook for ten minutes. Rub through a fine sieve and use.

BROWN SAUCE

To make a brown sauce, place four tablespoons of fat in a frying pan and add three tablespoons of flour. Stir until brown. Brown until a very dark color and then add one cup of stock or water. Stir until the mixture is perfectly smooth and at the boiling point for three minutes. Season as desired.

AMERICAN SAUCE

To make a sauce American take

One-half cup of thick cream sauce,
One-half cup of stewed tomatoes,
One tablespoon of grated onion,
One teaspoon of salt,
One teaspoon of paprika,
One tablespoon of grated cheese.

Blend and put through the fine sieve. Serve hot.

CREAM SAUCE

Place one cup of milk in saucepan and add three level tablespoons of flour. Stir with a fork or egg-beater until well mixed and then bring to a boil. Cool for three minutes and then stir constantly. Remove from the fire and use.

BOHEMIAN SAUCE

One cup of thick cream sauce,
Juice of one-half lemon,
One teaspoon of paprika,
One teaspoon of salt,
One tablespoon of fresh grated horseradish.

Beat to mix and then serve either hot or cold.

CANADIAN SAUCE

Place in a saucepan

Two grated onions,
One green pepper,
Two tomatoes, chopped very fine.

Cook slowly until soft, and then cool and add

Six tablespoons of salad oil,
Three tablespoons of vinegar,
One-quarter teaspoon of mustard,
One-half teaspoon of pepper,
One teaspoon of salt,
One-quarter teaspoon of sugar.

Mix thoroughly and serve cold over the fish.

HORSERADISH SAUCE

Add two tablespoons of grated horseradish and one tablespoon of Worcestershire sauce to either cream sauce or brown sauce.

MEXICAN CHILI SAUCE

Split open and then remove the seeds from one dozen chilis (green peppers). Now scrape the three or four veins to remove seeds that run through the pepper lengthwise. Now drop them into boiling water for fifteen minutes. Remove the skin and chop fine. Place four tablespoons of oil in an iron frying pan and add one-half cup of finely chopped onions. Cook slowly until tender, taking care not to brown. Now add two tablespoons of flour. Blend well and then add the chilis and

Two cups of tomato pulp rubbed through a fine sieve,
One cup of boiling water.

Simmer slowly until thick, smooth sauce. Season with salt to taste. Rub hand with salad oil, before preparing the peppers, to prevent burns.

BEVERAGES

To prepare chocolate as a beverage it is necessary to boil or cook it thoroughly. The mere fact of pouring boiling water or milk upon the cocoa will not cook it sufficiently.

HOW TO PREPARE CHOCOLATE

The Mexican epicure long ago discovered that to make chocolate successfully, it is necessary to beat it continually and he thus perfected a chocolate whip which is a wooden beater with a number of wooden rings fastened to it; when this is used to stir the chocolate it churns the mixture to a froth.

The French use a number of switches, bound into a whip. The American housewife uses a flat wire whip for this purpose.

Cocoa.—Place in a saucepan three-fourths cup of water and two level teaspoons of cocoa for each cup of cocoa desired. Bring to a boil and then cook for five minutes. Beat continually, then add one-fourth cup of scalded milk for each cup of cocoa. Bring to a boil again and then serve.

Chocolate.—Use three ounces of chocolate to one quart of water. Cut the chocolate fine and then add water and stir constantly. Bring to a boil and cook for ten minutes. Add one cup of scalded cream and then bring again to boiling point and serve. One tablespoon of whipped cream may be added to each cup just before serving.

HOW TO BREW A CUP OF TEA

From an old tea merchant in London I received my instructions for making a perfect cup of tea. First rinse out the teapot with cold water and then fill it with boiling water, and let stand while you bring the water intended for the tea to a boil. Just before the water boils, turn out the water in the teapot and wipe dry. Then add the tea leaves and pour on the freshly boiled water. Cover the pot with a tea cosy or wrap in a towel and let stand exactly seven minutes. The tea is now ready to drink. This will give you a delicious drink of ambrosia that will delight the heart of true lovers of a good cup of tea.

The use of a cosy for the teapot is to hold the heat in the pot and thus prevent quick cooling. Use one level teaspoon of tea to each one-half pint of water. Measure the water before boiling. The water must be poured on the tea immediately upon reaching the boiling point. After boiling for two minutes or longer the water quickly loses its natural gases.

COFFEE

Many varieties abound in the market. Among the best is the Arabian, with Liberian and Maragogipo closely following. After the coffee is harvested the quality and the value depend on the care in curing and packing. Brazil supplies the United States with about 80 per cent, of all the coffee used. Mexico and Central America together furnish about 17 per cent., thus leaving about 3 per cent. from foreign countries.

Various brands of coffee known by the housewife are:

Mocha,
Java,
Rio,
Santa Bourbon,
Santa,
Maracaibo,
Bogota,
Peaberry.

The first named are the most expensive, the last named the cheapest. The word "blend" when used with coffee means a mixing of two or more varieties, producing a coffee of various strengths and of a smooth, mellow flavor.

After the coffee is roasted it should be kept in air-tight cans. Grinding is the next important step, and this must be just right to get the full strength. Coffee coarsely ground is not desirable, as it requires a long time to infuse and is therefore wasteful. A medium fine grind will be found practical for those who use the old-style coffee pot. To filter, using the percolator, the coffee should be quite fine. The water falls continually over the coffee and produces a uniform cup.

How to make good coffee, using the old-fashioned coffeepot: Place one level tablespoon of medium finely ground coffee in the pot for every cup desired; add the water and bring quickly to the boiling point. Stir with a spoon and then add a small pinch of salt and four tablespoons of cold water to settle the grounds. Let it stand in a warm place for five minutes; then serve.

Percolator method: Place three-quarters of a level tablespoon of finely ground coffee in a percolator for each cup desired. Add the water and then place the pot on the fire. Let the coffee filter just four minutes after the first pumping of the water in the glass top shows a coffee color. This will produce an even, uniform cup of stimulating beverage.

COFFEE AU LAIT

French breakfast coffee: Make the coffee by the method desired, making only one-half the usual quantity. Now heat to the boiling point sufficient milk to fill each cup one-half full. When ready to serve, pour the hot milk in the cup and then fill it with coffee.

COFFEE NOIR

This coffee is usually drunk from the demi-tasse. Therefore, it should be of superior strength, usually one and one-quarter tablespoons are allowed of very finely ground coffee for every two cups. It is percolated until the liquid is very strong and is rich black in color; this takes, usually, from eight to ten minutes after the coffee first shows its color in the glass top of the percolator.

EPICUREAN CREOLE COFFEE

Many of the old Spanish and French grandees, who were the forefathers of the Franco-Spanish new world city, New Orleans, brought with them the beautiful china coffee pot of yesteryear. The making of the after-dinner coffee was an art indeed.

The pot was filled with hot water and then set in a pail of boiling water to keep warm while the coffee was milled. Generally it was roasted fresh every day. It was ground into a fine flour, then tied in a piece of thin, fine muslin. The water was drained from the heated pot and the coffee was placed in it. Then fresh boiling water was poured in. The spout and top were closely covered with a napkin and the pot returned to the pail, containing sufficient boiling water to keep the pot hot. It was placed before the fire to brew; this usually took from ten to fifteen minutes. The coffee was ready and its delicious aroma and flavor amply repaid one for the time and trouble taken to make it.

COFFEE A LA CREME

Coffee made in the usual manner and then served with plain and whipped cream.

TURKISH COFFEE

The coffee for this style is ground into a fine flour, and is then covered with cold water, brought to the boiling point, sweetened and served without straining or filtering. Russian coffee is heavy and black and is frequently served with a slice of lemon.

SUMMER DRINKS

A cool drink, with plenty of ice tinkling in the glass, refreshes and invigorates one at the close of a warm day. The housewife may prepare with little trouble many delicious fruit flavors from fresh fruits that can be quickly turned into thirst-quenching beverages, by adding ice and a little carbonated water.

Plain carbonated water may be purchased in either pint or quart bottles; and if a good cork is used to stop the opening of the bottles, after removing the caps, it may be used at intervals, providing it is kept on ice.

PARISIAN TEA

Place two teaspoonfuls of tea in a pitcher and pour over it one cup of boiling water. Cover closely and let stand for one-half hour. Drain and then place in the ice box until needed.

To serve—place four tablespoons of the tea infusion in a tall glass and add

Juice of one-half lemon,
One-half cup of crushed ice,
Three mint leaves,

and fill with carbonated water.

Use pulverized sugar to sweeten if desired.

CURRANT SLING

Place one box of currants in a saucepan and add three cups of water. Bring to a boil, mashing with potato masher. Cook for fifteen minutes and then strain. Add two cups of sugar and bring to a boil. Cook for five minutes and then cool. Place one-half of the currant syrup in a tall glass and add

One-half cup of crushed ice,
One tablespoon of lemon juice,
Six mint leaves,

and fill with carbonated water.

PINEAPPLEADE

Pare and grate one pineapple. Place in a saucepan and add

Two cups of sugar,
Two cups of water.

Bring to a boil and then simmer slowly for fifteen minutes. Cool and then add

One pint of crushed ice,
One cup of carbonated water,
Juice of two lemons.

EGG LEMONADE

Place the yolk of an egg in a small bowl and add

Three tablespoons of pulverized sugar,
Two tablespoons of lemon juice,
One-half cup of ice-cold water.

Beat to mix and then pour into tall thin glasses and add stiffly beaten white of egg, folding in carefully. Add four tablespoons of crushed ice and fill the glass with carbonated water. Orange juice may be used in place of the lemon juice.

MINT CUP

Place three sprigs of mint in a cup and add two tablespoons of sugar and crush. Now add

One drop of essence of peppermint,
One drop of essence of cloves,
One-half cup of crushed ice,

and fill with carbonated water.

GINGER ALE CUP

Place in a saucepan

Juice of one lemon,
Grated rind of one-quarter lemon,
One cup of sugar.

Simmer slowly until the sugar melts into the syrup. To use: Place three tablespoons of this prepared syrup in a tall thin glass and add

One-half cup of shaved ice,
One sprig of mint,
One-half cup of ginger ale,

and fill with carbonated water.

www.ingramcontent.com/pod-product-compliance
Lightning Source LLC
Chambersburg PA
CBHW081622100526
44590CB00021B/3552